# DATE DUE

| SEP 1 8 2013 | |
|---|---|
| | |
| | |
| | |
| | |
| | |
| | |
| | |
| | |
| | |
| | |
| | |
| | |
| | |
| | |

BRODART, CO.                    Cat. No. 23-221

# The Inner World of a
# Suicidal Youth

# The Inner World of a Suicidal Youth

What Every Parent and Health Professional Should Know

MILLIE OSBORNE, M.D.

PRAEGER

Westport, Connecticut
London

**Library of Congress Cataloging-in-Publication Data**

Osborne, Millie, 1963–
  The inner world of a suicidal youth : what every parent and health
professional should know / Millie Osborne.
    p. ; cm.
  Includes bibliographical references and index.
  ISBN 978-0-313-34855-6 (alk. paper)
  1. Youth—Suicidal behavior—United States—Case studies. 2. Suicide—
United States—Case studies. I. Title.
  [DNLM: 1. Adolescent—Personal Narratives. 2. Suicide—
psychology—Personal Narratives. WM 165 O81i 2007]
  RJ506.S9O83 2008
  362.280835—dc22        2007038054

British Library Cataloguing in Publication Data is available.

Library of Congress Catalog Card Number: 2007038054
ISBN: 978-0-313-34855-6

First published in 2008

Praeger Publishers, 88 Post Road West, Westport, CT 06881
An imprint of Greenwood Publishing Group, Inc.
www.praeger.com

Printed in the United States of America

∞™

The paper used in this book complies with the
Permanent Paper Standard issued by the National
Information Standards Organization (Z39.48–1984).

10  9  8  7  6  5  4  3  2  1

For Electra and all children of the world

# Contents

*buying diapers, food, and clothing and babysitting whenever the mother went to work. Her first nine years seemed to be jubilant. She did exceptionally well in school and made friends easily with her gentle demeanor and kindheartedness. By the time she was ten, she was reading at a high school level, solving math problems at a middle school level, and building a large circle of friendships. Electra was talented like everyone's child and anyone's child.*

*Her mother traveled for entertainment, often leaving her grandparents with full responsibility for the child. When Electra turned eight, her mother announced her plans to move out of the grandparents' house in New York and into a Manhattan apartment with a boyfriend. Though the details and motives remain unclear, the move was coincident with rising discord between her mother and her grandparents. The stated reason for the move was to improve Electra's educational experience by enrolling her in a special gifted and talented program located on the west side of Manhattan. The grandparents objected to the move, expressing concerns about Electra residing with a man they did not know and the difficulty of continuing their on-demand babysitting care when Electra's mother traveled for days or sometimes weeks at a time. Despite the family's objections, shortly after Electra's eighth birthday she and her mother relocated to Manhattan. Two years after that, she and her mother moved out of the apartment with the boyfriend and into their own apartment in the same school district.*

*Her grandparents were regular visitors to the downtown location and brought Electra back home to live with them when her mother left for a trip to Singapore one day, stating that she would return in a week. It was several months before her mother returned. During that time, her grandparents made daily trips from the Bronx to her school in Manhattan and took Electra with them to church events on the weekends. The mother called periodically, but the family still worried. No one knew why her mother was taking so long to return home. No one knew why she had left. Most of all, Electra did not understand, and the child's longing was not to be comforted by grandparents, aunts, or uncles.*

*The grandparents continued to pay the rent on Electra and her mother's apartment until her mother returned from Singapore almost eight months later. Now twelve years old, Electra's joy was obvious; any other emotion was not. Even when her mother's sickness was revealed, joy in her mother's presence was the only emotion apparent from Electra's demeanor.*

*By the standards of most, Electra had a majestic beauty. During puberty, she blossomed into a taller-than-average adolescent, slender, well figured, and always catching the males' stares when she entered a room. Her soft skin saw little of adolescent acne, so she always appeared radiant and stunning. Her demeanor was genteel always, and she had kind words for all. She openly objected to anyone using vulgar* words in her presence. Her behavior toward her family was always respectful and kind. As she entered one of the best science and technology high schools in the country, she was faced with a major life challenge: the realization that her mother would not recover from her sickness. She was very close to her mother and often referred to her grandfather as her daddy.

As Electra grew up she began asking about her real daddy, prompting her grandmother to investigate the identity and whereabouts of Electra's biological father. The grandmother was concerned and believed that investigating would help what appeared to be a young girl's longing.

The grandmother discovered that before Electra's birth, her mother's boyfriend had denied being the father on the grounds that he was diagnosed as being sterile as a child. Yet some years later, the grandmother discovered that the boyfriend had since married and had a new baby with his wife. The resemblance of Electra to this man was also suggestive, even when another of her mother's ex-boyfriends claimed to be the father. While the grandmother's investigation resulted in some child support and, later, visitations, Electra's mother was furious about the grandmother's intrusive actions. While this incident did not begin the discord between mother and grandmother, it made the relationship more troublesome than before. When arguments erupted between Electra's mother and grandmother, Electra remained silent, always respectful and loving to both.

Reading another person's diary can feel like peeping into someone's bedroom window. Most people are curious to see yet don't want to infringe upon another's privacy, lest someone do the same to them. Electra kept a meticulous diary for so many years, for so many reasons. Her gifted beauty and intelligence made her everyone's child—the child everyone hopes for, with the limitless potential that everyone wants. If such a fate can happen to everyone's child then it can happen to anyone's child, unless we understand how and why. Families often don't talk, let alone write about such loss, perhaps because the pain never wears off enough to do so. But while family secrets may shield some of the pain, they leave little from which to learn. Electra's giftedness and despair are not to be viewed with heroic mystique that vulnerable minds crave, for her gifts were engulfed by pain, a different kind of pain that erodes promising talent. The enigma begins with Clio.

APRIL 25, 1995

Dear Clio,

It's twelve o'clock in the morning on a school night and I'm sitting on the toilet writing. I know I'm going to be dead tired in the morning, but who cares. Grandma lurks outside the bathroom door, so I'm staying put. I was kind of numb all day, a state I am unfortunately finding myself in more and

JUNE 3, 1995

Dear Clio,

I have one question left on my geometry and have lost all will to finish it tonight. Emma all of a sudden started speaking to me again. I think I'm over Steven. I sure hope so because he doesn't even know I'm alive in that way. Grandma brought up the church issue again and I changed the subject so hopefully she'll just forget about it. I have to get fourteen dollars together now so that I can pay Columbia. Things have to change. I'm going to pay BMG and cancel my membership, pay off all of my subscriptions and be done with that mess. I'm going to buy the six CDs from Columbia then cancel my membership. The way I see it, buying services where they don't have any special sales, will be enough for me. I'm going to write mom a letter with the amount that I need now, and a budget. I have to clean up my act now! Grandma lent me two curling irons. I don't see why she couldn't just give me one because she has like six of them, but the loan is appreciated. She is so cheap. Aunt Deborah is right; this is not by any means normal. Grandma is obsessed with having things. She bought flannel pillowcases just because they were $3.00. What the hell sense does that make? My bio project has officially died. I think that I'll lock my door tonight to prevent Grandma from making me go to church tomorrow. I'm an agnostic, they're just going to have to deal with that. Mom started bitching about her grave. I looked when I came to see her yesterday. She should understand that these aren't happy visits. I'm sick of everyone bitching about my damn attitude. F——k them all! I can't be sad when I am and I'm not happy so forget that, and if I hide my feelings I'm being cold. I don't like it here and I want to go home. But I don't have a home anymore so I guess that there's no point in wishing for it. What's left beside bills and broken hearts? She's not going to make it. It's obvious to me. Maybe instead of suicide, I'll run away and become a hooker and die of AIDS before I'm twenty. If the next say ten years of my life could go on without me knowing it I'd be happy. Twenty-five seems like such a happy but distant age. I wish that I hadn't invited Jolie or Amanda to the beach house. I want to be alone with someone. Grandma is always butting into everything; it is so damn obnoxious. I'm so tired and weak and sickly feeling. I can't talk to anyone here because no one here has an answer. They use the Bible as the answer to everything. However I love my grandfather with all my heart. I'm not sure if I love my grandmother anymore but I hope so. She is so mean to grandpa that it's hard to love her. On the upside, turns out Trans has a new album out. It's called Keoul and the Kings of Spain but it was sold out at the store. I wish I could die. William and Renee look so happy together. I want to be happy like that. But I doubt that I ever will be because I'm like guy repellant! I'm going to bed! Kevin rules! Love ya. Electra

JUNE 4, 1995
    Dear Clio,
    Oh no! If I don't get a check for Columbia by Tuesday I'm screwed big time. Looks like I'm going to be doing some groveling. Mom might be coming home tomorrow. I'm pretty neutral feeling about it because sadly enough, I really don't care. Lately I try to focus on anything but her. Tomorrow I'm going to experiment with the curling irons. I did eight pages of Jolie's book tonight. It was fun. I finally killed that little bug. I'm so happy about that. I wish that school would hurry up and damn it! Everyday seems to drag on. Actually, we only have nine days left but it seems like forever. Amanda is so lucky. Yet another guy likes her. It's just not fair. What do guys find irresistible about her? I bet Steven likes her too. He's probably pissed at me for liking him because that would make it kind of inappropriate to ask her out. I don't blame him for not liking me but it hurts all the same. Maybe he wasn't the guy in that wonderful dream; actually I could've sworn that he had black hair, like whom? Maybe I'll meet him next year. My memory is shot. I can't remember when I last had my period so I don't know if it's late or not. I just realized that both of my story characters have gone off the air. I'm praying that Jodie comes back in another his series. Since Full House went down in that ratings and our first video is off the charts, and the mystery cruise fell off the video charts after one week, would that indicate that the Olsen twins' popularity is finally going down? I sure hope so. Why do people keep calling hip-hop a mega-smash? I'll have to look into this. I can't wait to get Billiard and TV Guide maybe 'Child's Play' will finally mention Raven Symone. Can't believe that Aunt Deborah was back on drugs and I can't believe that grandma told me—what a bitchy horrible mean thing to do and I hate it. Well I must be going. Gwen rules! Love ya bye! Love, Electra

JUNE 5, 1995
    Dear Clio,
    I hate it here so much. I got a cell card from school, and Grandma is going to be a bitch and go to my school to straighten this out. I'm so angry I could cry. I need to get out of here. I hate her so much sometimes. What an obnoxious bitch! I want to go home. I want to run away. I want to die. Life is too hard. I just can't take it. Why can't my life be easy or at least happy? Why does god choose to screw me over all the time? I swear I can't take it anymore. Suicide is looking better and better, but what about my children

think I can deal with that and it's not fair. He's inserting himself as this power figure and it's not appreciated to say the least. I don't want a father, I want a mother, but Aunt Susan doesn't want to be my mother. I'm going from being broke and suicidal at grandma's house to being broke and suicidal at Uncle Phillip's house. Will this hell ever end? I just want to be happy, that's all I ask. I won't be getting anything new for a long time. Uncle Phillip only has eyes for Aunt Susan. There will be no more shopping sprees. No more twenties on Fridays to go out with my friends. No more surprise gifts. No more I love you before I go to bed. Now no one worries about me when I go off to school, or downtown with my friends. No one cares. There's no one left to talk to honestly, no one that takes my views seriously. All that is gone. I wish that I were two. All I have are memories. I would give anything to have mom back. Unfortunately, anything just isn't enough. Love Electra

FEBRUARY 13, 1996

Dear Clio,

It's been ages since I last wrote but now fortunately I'm still alive. I go to the Park School here in Maryland. I met a wonderful woman named Wendy Owen and I have a boyfriend named Adam. Both of them are causing me a lot of pain. I don't want to be going out with Adam. He's like a brother to me not a boyfriend. Besides that I find him physically repulsive. Whenever he kisses me I want to wretch. But he's such a nice guy; I don't have the heart to break up with him. Dr. Owen knows all of my deepest darkest secrets (well almost) but I'm starting to think that she doesn't care. I love her with all my heart but she has no obligation to me so she can string me along as much as she likes. I also have a friend named Elizabeth who, like me, hates herself and wants to die. However I think that her death would actually be a great loss. I remember when I was eight years old and some guy fondled me at a party. That screwed me up mentally and sexually. Adam knows but he will not respect the fact that when men touch me it scares me. I haven't told Dr. Owen. She knows that I'm suicidal and claims to care but she won't help me. If only I had a method. I'm thinking caffeine pills. They're nonprescription and they're cheap. Unfortunately the death is not pleasant. Somehow the idea of going into convulsions does not appeal to me. But I might try it. If I can find no other accessible method I don't think it would be any great loss. I looked at myself in the mirror one day and thought 'you stupid piece of sh——t.' It's no way to live. I want to be with my mother. I'm so sad all of the time. Adam says that I should live for other people yet he thinks that authors shouldn't have to bear the burden of writing for others. My feelings aren't important. I will find a way out of here. Love Electra

FEBRUARY 14, 1996
   Dear Clio,
   Today is Valentine's Day. I have to do something about Adam. I hate it when I get annoyed with him because he's such a nice guy but I hate being coddled. His flattering is starting to piss me off. It's me I know that. I am so sexually screwed up because of what happened to me freaky seven years ago. Everything he does just bothers me. Yet I feel sad every time I realize that he's leaving. I feel so alone a lot of the time. My new suicide plan is caffeine and alcohol. The combination might keep off the convulsions or at least dull the pain. Now all I need is time. I don't want my aunt and uncle home when I do it. Today we watched this really disturbing movie on slavery called 'Sankobe.' It was pretty weird. I feel so fat today. I need to find something to speed up my metabolism. If I could give up food I would. In fact I'm going to find a way. That's my new goal. I don't want to start the whole laxative mess again but I might. I hate myself so much that I really don't mind destroying my body. Fat is an added discomfort. I'm going to kill myself during my second week of spring break. Yes that makes sense. My plan is to take 24 caffeine pills, 20 ibuprofens 6 Nyquil and some kind of strong alcoholic beverage like whiskey. All of these will have to be taken rapidly in my room. Actually instead of the Nyquil or in addition to it I am going to take a box of Nytol. Perhaps I will die in my sleep. That's good news. Well I'm going to plan. Love Electra

MARCH 11, 1996
   Dear Clio,
   For the first time in years I don't have an incredible urge to die. I'm in Jamaica and I haven't been dwelling on my problems all day like I usually do. I guess that realizing that I was almost raped when I was five, kind of puts things in perspective. It explains why I hate sleeping with people, which is something I've always wondered. I told Dr. Owen and she said 'that's amazing.' I told Aunt Susan and she said 'wow.' I feel like some sideshow freak. Anyway, it's beautiful here. It's actually warm, a feeling I haven't experienced in months. I've been sick all winter with some unidentified bug. Hopefully this weather will do me some good. No one has inquired about my age so I'm going to be doing a sh——tload of drinking. Sounds good to me. I found out that I'm part Irish; that explains a lot. I don't know

what this feeling is but it might be happiness. I've kind of forgotten what that feels like. Could I be getting better? It seems like it's been so long since mom died. But it hasn't been. And I'm a horrible person for feeling better so soon, right? I don't know. The thing that hurts me the most is the memories of her last days. She fell so low. I didn't recognize her. I hope she knows how much I love her. She's not going to be there for my sixteenth birthday. That's really going to hurt. She was looking forward to it. We were going to do something special. God I miss her. Love Electra

*This was Electra's last entry for two years. She had discovered an alternate outlet very different from writing. The quiescent ideation about suicide methods that began at age eleven had gained its own momentum once verbalized to family and friends for the first time. She had never told the mother she loved about these thoughts that she replayed over and over in her writing. She was a teenage girl grieving the death of her mother. Loss and abandonment were pains that had left her powerless and more obsessed with self-demise. Yet between February and March 1996, she seemed to experience an almost miraculous recovery. What Electra did not write about was her first open suicide attempt while living with her aunt and uncle. She decided not to share with Clio that it was the suicide attempt in February that led to a change in her uncle's plans to go to Jamaica with his wife alone. The loss of her mother to the grave and the pending loss of her aunt and uncle to Jamaica were too overwhelming for her to write about. This time she swallowed several nonprescription pain pills, staggered from her bedroom to her uncle, and told him she was trying to die. The result was her first psychiatric hospitalization, appointments with a therapist and a psychiatrist, a prescription for an antidepressant, and being able to go with her aunt and uncle to Jamaica. When, in a family therapy session with the psychiatrist, Electra revealed her memories of sexual abuse at ages five and eight, she seemed to experience a renewal from the effect this information had on her family; it was healing on one level, empowering on another.*

*Electra was certain about the details surrounding the abuse at age eight, but she could never recall details about what her mother told her had occurred at age five. Until she was eight, Electra lived with her grandparents and was often under their watch. When Electra was five her mother, following an argument with a sibling, began shouting accusations that the family had molested Electra. That Electra could only recall the alleged trauma as her mother told it to her suggests that these were planted, not real, memories. The abuse just before her ninth birthday was real, not imagined. Even knowing the truth years later could not undo the childhood belief planted by the person she trusted most. Real and planted, she was still victimized twice.*

*So her uncle and aunt, feeling guilty about going away, arranged to take her with them. They hoped that the warm weather might help her heal. Her March entry*

to Clio marked the beginning of a confident period sustained by considerable sacrifice from her family, who were unable to afford her trip to Jamaica with them because they were already paying thousands of dollars for her private high school. Often, to appease Electra, family and friends had to sacrifice around monetary matters. As she honestly reports to Clio, she has no control over her spending, even though she was brilliant in mathematics and business finance. What she doesn't tell Clio, but what is apparent in how she behaved toward her family, is that she wanted complete control over other people's money. As a result, her Aunt Deborah went into considerable debt to appease Electra's spending habits; and her Uncle Phillip and Aunt Susan, between paying for her education and mail-order subscriptions and now expecting their own child, were beginning to question what was happening.

During the summer of 1996, Electra was invited on an oceanfront vacation with her mother's sister, Aunt Ellie, and her husband and children. She was eager to go since she had few summer activities and was getting bored with helping her Aunt Susan, who was now on bedrest with the pregnancy. The family beach trip was scheduled for a full week with a full array of activities. However, Electra announced on the first day which restaurants she wanted to eat in and which activities she wanted to do, none of which was part of the family's vacation plans and all of which were the most expensive in the resort area. When her uncle reminded her about the family activities, indicating that she would join the family's plans and not the other way around, she became emotionally withdrawn and angry for the remainder of the day. By evening she was in tears, sobbing about missing her mother and not to be consoled even when her young cousins tried to embrace her. In the morning she refused breakfast because it was not at the restaurant she had selected and remained near tears and noncommunicative for much of the morning, until she spotted a souvenir in a storefront and asked her aunt if she would buy it for her. After the aunt purchased the item, Electra's entire demeanor changed. She smiled and began talking to her cousins; she even ate lunch, even though it was not at the restaurant she wanted. The entire week vacillated in this fashion, as the aunt and uncle were invested parents and persisted in the effort to set appropriate limits on Electra's attempts to spend their money and dominate their vacation. They were equally invested in circumventing Electra's daily attempts to monopolize their attention to the point of neglecting their three children, her cousins. While Electra had not demonstrated overt cruelty toward her cousins, she was generally dismissive of their existence or their right to enjoy the family vacation. Electra's narcissism became more apparent each day, as did her attempts to all but ruin the trip. Her aunt and uncle were aware that her behavior had already put one aunt in financial and emotional turmoil, and they included warm hugs and gentle discussion in their attempts to help her enjoy herself. After all, it was just shortly after the first anniversary of her *incident on Jessica was as profound as the ancient victory described in the tale of Oedipus. The developing and high acuity brain of this small child would always perceive an unseen bond with her father and assume a warrior's stance with her mother. In some way, the mother would always blame Jessica for that painful moment of humiliation, always questioning her husband's love for her, always loving the child yet painfully aware of the child's love-hate feelings toward her, always.*

*But Juliet, the mother, did not know about Jessica's surreptitious tendency to deliberately poison her siblings against her. Jessica was a born leader, very intelligent and charismatic. She spared no detail in maligning her mother to the younger siblings; she knew that young minds were more suggestible so she did not use this tactic with her two older brothers. Jessica focused on Julie because she saw that Julie was more eager to believe. Even though Ellie and Phillip were younger than Julie, they refused to accept Jessica's views about their mother. So even after Jessica married at the young age of nineteen and moved to another state, she remained in constant contact with Julie thus sustaining the discord between mother and daughters. While Julie grew bonded to Jessica, most of her siblings kept a comfortable distance from Jessica's ongoing critiques of their mother. And so was the undercurrent of life at home for Julie.*

*Her performance in school was exceptional both socially and academically. Julie skipped the eighth grade and, by her thirteenth birthday, had received a full scholarship to a prestigious boarding school about an hour's drive from the family home. Her parents were reluctant to have their daughter leave home at such a young age but also wanted Julie to have the best education to match her brilliance. Julie also was excited about going and so she did. After she moved into the dorm she did not expect the feelings of homesickness that came over her. She called home often and her parents drove out to visit her often. It was only many years later that the parents would find out why Julie had stopped calling home; they would learn that Jessica had intercepted their visits with messages to Julie that their parents sent her away because they wanted her out of the home. Jessica had convinced Julie that their parents did not want her; she told her that their mother had said this because she had so many children and was glad to see one go elsewhere. Their mother never said this but the lie and all of the distorted truths had changed Julie for life. Suddenly Julie was asking her parents not to visit. Instead of calling home, she followed the path of an abandoned child. Her new school friends became her family. These friends were the daughters of millionaires, all accustomed to making use of the less fortunate people of society, people like Julie.*

*She was a slender, sultry beauty who walked with poise and grace, speaking the king's English with impeccable diction. She was welcomed into the rich girls' naughty dorm club and followed the lead into a high society call girl operation that paired her and several other high school girls with wealthy married men. It was long after the fact that her parents figured out what was happening to their daughter. When they visited Julie on campus and questioned the expensive garments in her closet and jewels on her chest she told them her girlfriends had given them to her. They questioned how she was paying for trips abroad during school breaks and she again told them it was her wealthy girlfriends. But her mother, more street smart than her father, never stopped investigating what her daughter was doing in return for the expensive trips and gifts. During Julie's junior year in high school, her parents paid her a surprise visit at school and discovered empty liquor bottles under her bed. When they asked their daughter what was going on, she threw a tantrum accusing her parents of butting into her life and informing them that it was none of their business. Her parents threatened to remove her from the school but were ambivalent about compromising an excellent education. In preparation for any further surprise visits from the parents, Julie developed a unique brand of secrecy and deceit, apologizing to her parents and presenting the image of an innocent daughter while continuing her drinking, smoking, and call girl operation with her wealthy friends.*

*She was much smarter than her grades reflected, but she passed all course work sufficient to graduate at only seventeen and get accepted into three prestigious colleges, though meager grades did not confer any scholarship offers. Once she moved back home the summer of her graduation, her double life was no longer easy to conceal. She changed the spelling of her name from Juliet to Juliette, perhaps to emphasize just how different she wanted to be from her mother. She would leave home in the morning, telling her parents she was looking for a summer job and would not return later that day. Often it was many days, sometimes weeks before her parents saw or heard from her again. The worry tormented her parents, as Julie never explained her disappearing acts or lies about returning and never apologized for her behavior. By mid-summer, her parents were forced into an ultimatum: Julie was either to be truthful with them about her disappearances and other activities or they would not fund a college education. Julie refused on the grounds that it was not their business. She did not go to college in 1978 or in 1979 when she met Thomas.*

*She was waitressing at a seafood restaurant in Manhattan when she first met him. Handsome, tall, and articulate, he had all of the familiar signs of a man with wealth; after all he came with the lunch crowd of silk patterned business suits. But unlike the other wealthy men she kept company with, this man was younger and single. Julie knew well how to charm and flatter as a natural seductress with natural beauty. Along with a sizeable tip, Thomas asked her out to dinner. Before that day was over, she knew that she wanted to marry this young rich man named Thomas even though it was really his father who was wealthy, and family money that he was in Manhattan to invest. Ten years Julie's senior, Thomas enjoyed life as a bachelor, all the while, her discussions with her daughter were more that of a companion than a mother. She made no attempt to make alternate plans for her daughter's future and never discussed any likelihood that the cancer would take her life. Indeed, her guidance to her only child was that of denial as she talked about future trips they would take abroad together. She did not want to die, she was not prepared to die, and she could not prepare Electra either. Taking the lead was not in her nature.*

*While her father drove Julie to and from doctor appointments and Electra to and from school, her mother, Juliet senior, was getting sick too. Who would have imagined that two tragedies could affect the same family at the same time? Gradually, the senior Juliet started to change. Her cooking tasted bland and she started to forget the words to hymns she had been performing for the church for over thirty years. She was a natural nurse. Since the age of ten when she cared for her dying stepmother she always tried to care for others. So her care for her dying daughter remained stellar even while her demeanor became more childlike. She remained sensitive and compassionate as her motherly love always was despite a slowly progressing dementia. She cleaned up Julie's vomit from the chemotherapy, bathed and dressed her when she was too weak to get out of bed. Though seeing and receiving such care, Julie and Electra believed Juliet's childlike expressions to be malevolent. Julie never knew that her mother was also very sick. Julie's mother had not been officially diagnosed at that point but the family was later to learn that she had Alzheimer's disease. The family was preoccupied with Julie's more rapidly deteriorating condition and did not recognize the mother's illness. But even with her memories and abilities starting to fade, Juliet knew that her daughter and namesake was dying and grieved silently along with her husband.*

parents. I don't think they realize how much I love them and enjoy their company. Aunt Deborah is easier to deal with and a lot of fun but I really like my parents too. I don't know how to show them that. I'm on a long high. It's been two days practically without a plunge. I think it's because I'm away from that hellhole. The one thing that bothers me is these combined assumptions and assaults on my character and my intentions. I do not feel like anybody owes me anything. I'm an orphan, why would I even assume that I was entitled to anything. It just doesn't make sense. Anyway this week will be okay, I hope. I feel bad about dragging Aunt Deborah all the way down here but it was very good to see her anyway. The Luvox I just took is giving me a stomachache. I don't think I'll be exercising tonight. Love Electra

*Some people write diaries as a comforting release of their most intimate and sincere thoughts. Others write because it is the only safe place to reflect on life without being judged. Some don't realize how this release ends up mapping out the most intricate elements of the mind. Electra maps out in her diary that it was her aunt and uncle who so wanted her to attend Wharton but it was her mother who idolized Wharton before she died. Electra had turned down several other schools to attend Wharton where she started out excelling in her courses, appearing to all to be adjusting well to college life. But the reality of a college workload and goal of Wall Street success clashed with Electra's ability to handle the stressful challenges involved. It was her mother who taught Electra to idolize status and money, believing that graduating from such a school would guarantee her daughter a life with both. Her aunt and uncle never directed Electra to attend Penn, as it was a decision Electra insisted on making without their input. What Electra told others and told her diary is often to be found at opposite ends of her mind's map. In reality, she was miserable because of her own decision influenced completely by the will of her mother. Electra's reflections about the college she chose, map out something she believes subconsciously even if the reality is very different.*

*There is a need to understand the significance of both what is written and what is not written as Electra mourns about her life and wishes for death. Nowhere in her dairy did she mention how sick her Aunt Susan was with the second pregnancy. While Electra sought to build an emotional defense for joining her aunt and uncle on their pending relocation to Florida, much like her victories in the Jamaica and France decisions, she completely dismissed her aunt's bedridden condition and imminent miscarriage. She does not allude to how her behavior during the aunt's first pregnancy stressed the family so much that it almost caused a miscarriage, death, of that child. She professes in her writings to love her Aunt Susan yet professes no concern about the aunt's well-being or that of her unborn child. The reader would not even know about the seriousness of the aunt's condition because Electra has dismissed its reality while her behavior proceeds to escalate.*

*Between January and March 1999, Aunt Susan's condition worsened to the point that she required assistance whenever she ambulated. They hired a caregiver to help her around the house and with their toddling daughter. That "weak woman" Electra took advantage of on March 8 was the bedridden aunt. For all of Electra's apparent behaviors, she not only did not seem to care about her aunt's health, she overwhelmed the household, risking the lives of both aunt and cousin. This real possibility did not seem to bother a person so preoccupied with taking her own life. After all, taking life or causing life to be lost was the mirror she looked into everyday. Her Uncle Phillip viewed Electra's behavior as a deliberate threat to the lives of his wife and unborn child. Whether subconscious or deliberate, his niece had engaged him in another battle of emotional blackmail that was destroying his family.*

*Because she maintained a convincing innocence and sincerity to the world, no one but her diaries knew that she entertained death on a daily basis. Each time Electra expressed her suicidal thoughts openly, the stakes were higher than before. She had reluctantly adjusted to having one child, Patricia, in the home but her actions suggested that she did not want another one. If her aunt lost the baby then she would more likely be included in their relocation plans; she was determined to be part of those plans no matter what she had to do or make happen. The kindness of her words and the lethality of her behavior toward her family were so contradictory that she enraged her uncle. As a result, the uncle did what most men would do when someone threatens the life of his family: he protected them.*

MARCH 10, 1999

Day two (or 1½) on Luvox: aside from the shaking hands and nausea, things are going well. I should have called Aunt Deborah but I didn't. I spent most of the day kind of groggy. Now I'm suffering from a peanut butter and hot chocolate induced stomachache. About this whole student health shrink thing what exactly am I supposed to get from this person? Aunt Ellie has already diagnosed me. Uncle Phillip took care of the prescription. I don't want to see another psychiatrist. My first one was bad enough. I'll have to discuss this with Aunt Ellie. I'm starting to suspect that my parents are almost as intimidated by me as I am by them. I don't know how to change that though. My aunt's going to do my hair tomorrow and I'm trying to think of things to talk to her about. I think she's so used to the never-ending discourse of the other Binets that she no longer feels the need to try with me. I don't like awkward silences but I always feel stupid trying to fill them. I'm already starting to get that back to hell ... I mean Penn, anxiety. I wish I could stay here for a few months. Actually I wish Aunt Deborah and I could run away somewhere and live a carefree life. She gets on my nerves sometimes but she also makes me happier than anyone. Unconditional love is something everyone needs despite what my uncle might think. He would not be nearly so confident without his wife. He can't put himself in my position because he never experienced anything like it, and I hope he never does. Aunt Ellie calls them strong people but look at them. They've led charmed lives untouched by much adversity. I'm not saying they're weak but what can I draw from a strength that can't even relate to my weaknesses. So instead I picture them as ideals that I strive for (for the most part) and I look to those that have been down this path for guidance. Love Electra

MARCH 11, 1999

Thursday already! I'm already dreading my return. Had a pretty unremarkable day except that I now have some possible bangs. I cut them myself, against my better judgment but Aunt Susan wouldn't do it. They're a bit shaggy but, oh well. The Excedrin and Luvox are both seeming to knock me out and it's only 1:44. I can't go to bed this early though, well actually it's not so much the time as much as the fact that I've got a lot of econ to read and, as you know, I'm not functional in the morning. I still haven't confided in anyone about my taking Excedrin to go to sleep. For some reason I don't want them to know that I really can't go to sleep on my own. It's ridiculous I know but it's true. So I don't think I'll be able to stay up much longer. Better at least find some interest in econ. Love Electra

MARCH 12, 1999

Three days till my birthday. I know I'm setting myself up for a big disappointment but I'm really looking forward to it. Not that nineteen is any big deal but things are looking up. I can already feel the Luvox kicking in. If I wasn't so damn sleepy all the time I'm sure the results would really shine through. I've been really shaky lately which is kind of worrisome. I don't want to alert the authorities just yet. I'm kind of mad at Aunt Ellie for not even giving me a chance to tell them about the relapse myself. She didn't even wait a whole day. Well what's done is done. I still haven't called Aunt Deborah, which I should have done a while ago. I think we're both feeling kind of embarrassed about the whole fiasco. I think I'll call her from Philly. I just realized how essential it is that I have a job in May. I've got bills to pay. Those credit cards were a huge mistake. I'm going over to Blockbuster tomorrow. I should have gone earlier this week. I've just been in a fog this week. Hopefully I'll be more awake than I have been, definitely too much Excedrin. I had dinner with Debbie and Doug and their kids. I still love talking to Debbie and Doug but I never know how to talk to their kids. Betty seems a little more normal than she used to be and Dana is still Dana. I think they're comparable to Rachel and Adelah from the Passion Bible. Well maybe Dana would be more like Ruth Mary but that seems like a rather morbid comparison. Anyway, it was a nice evening and they of course showered me with birthday gifts. I'm not sure if I was supposed to wait to open them. If so oops! Anyway I love that family. They make me feel so special. Love Electra

MARCH 15, 1999

Well the call is your money or your life and suddenly I'm starting to value mine. And maybe the knife in the outlet or the plummet off the balcony is the only way to save myself. How can I choose between my aunt who loves me and whom I love more than anyone and my college education and the possible future it holds? The very idea of calling my father for help makes me cringe almost as much as the thoughts of signing that evil thing. So is this where it ends, in a burst of flames and excruciating pain? I suppose it would be fast enough and that is of the utmost importance. The walls are finally collapsing on me. The only thing I've ever had was my autonomy and he wants to take that away (the Bastard!). So how can I go on? I cannot be enslaved and live my life. I fought hard for it too. It may sound as if I'm giving in easily but on the contrary if that were true I would have died in some gruesome manner in my exile at grandma's house. It is time for me to join my mother wherever she is. We weren't meant to be apart. I knew it before she died. These past three and a half years have been a waste of precious time and resources. I'll probably hang around a few days though so this isn't quite goodbye. Also, fate might intervene and prevent my going but I think that I have reached the end of my rope. It's a shame that it was made so short. This is to all the teens who have jumped into the great beyond. I understand. If no one else does, I understand. On this my birthday I begin my mental preparations to take the plunge. The fear and the hurt have finally won. I think I'll have to write a long letter of explanation to my dear aunt and then to the others, and then maybe to Kathy. I just got a lovely birthday note from Dan. They won't understand ... they make me so sad to leave. Love Electra

MARCH 17, 1999

Well the crisis continues. I've calmed down a bit. Not feeling too suicidal anymore. I just need to talk to him and it is so hard. I'm rehearsing it in my head over and over, actually thinking of writing it down but he is so scary to me. Aunt Ellie can face him, but I'm just not that brave, never have been. I've spent my life cowering away from ill-tempered men so this is years and years of cowering that I need to work out. But I am not relinquishing control of my life to humor anyone at this point. I'm in too deep. We need to communicate, and we need to help me budget but this is simply not the way. If he refuses to finance my education then so be it. Suddenly I'm not so afraid anymore. Anyway dawn approaches so I'm going to try to get some sleep. Hopefully my father will turn up and then I'll have at least one unbiased opinion. I really wonder where he is. Love Electra

MARCH 19, 1999

I'm examining my pathetic self, hating life and wondering exactly how I can right this wrong. My whole family has turned against me while meanwhile sucking away my very core. I've become entirely too dependent on them. When Mom was alive I was this independent, if troubled, spirit. Now I'm a very frustrated corpse to be. I'm going to give modeling a try if not only to get from under my uncle's thumb. He doesn't need any more stresses in his life. I wish, for his sake and mine that I could disappear. I've decided to move to California after college. I need to get away. All Aunt Deborah can do is spout clichés. Aunt Ellie is the only one who says anything comforting and constructive. The simple fact of the matter is that Uncle Phillip doesn't like me and there's no way to change that. I don't make his days any brighter. All I am is a burden. I'm seriously considering swallowing a thumbtack or something, perhaps the fork in the socket. There's no reason for me to be here. I'm a waste of oxygen. I wanted to give life to a child but now I don't think I'd be a very good mother. I need to leave this place. I can't even picture the future anymore. I have utterly failed in my life and it is painful to live. I know it would hurt a few people but I am of too little consequence to leave any scars. The Lord is my Shepherd and I soon hope to join him in his kingdom of heaven. Now I truly believe. Love Electra

MARCH 22, 1999

Well this has been an eventful weekend. Kelly got seriously smashed last night and puked and wandered for a while. I feel horrible about the whole thing. I knew she was drinking too much, but I guess I thought she'd feel better afterwards. But instead I feel like she's self destructing but so am I just a little more calmly. I think she's what's keeping me here. I do this all the time, just grow entirely too attached to people. I just think that my death might destroy her. I'm guessing that at that point I wouldn't care but right now I do and before that bag goes over my head I've got to make sure that she's going to be okay. I'm not sure if I should tell her what I'm going to do beforehand. She might try to stop me although I'm sure that she'd understand the whole situation is just a mess. This was to be my last weekend. I can't worry about my uncle because I know he'll be okay. But I won't. I'm not equipped to deal with this stuff or anything for that matter. I'd really like to go before my math midterm. I don't want everyone thinking I did it because of a test. That would just further tarnish my reputation. I'm not sure if Em will care too much. I am really curious about the hereafter. I'm seriously wondering if I should stick around till after Virginia Beach. I don't want to ruin it for them. But at the same time I don't think this can wait. I'm a little nervous but not too afraid. I think I'll be able to go through with it. Undone by a website. How ironic. Love Electra

MARCH 31, 1999

Well I didn't chicken out, well at least not consciously. The sleeping pills disoriented me instead of putting me to sleep, so I stumbled into the lounge and was found out by Emily and others. So I spent another week in hell (i.e. the psych ward at HUP). I lied like I have never lied before and they let me out. Now I'm trying to figure out when and how to finally end this. The pain is too great and I've already been abandoned by my parents. So sticking around will never be worth it. I'll miss Patricia but maybe it's good that she'll be engraved in my memory as the cherubic two year old she is. God I love that child. I'm glad she's too young to really miss me. Kelly presents an interesting problem. On the one hand I think I'm a horrible influence on her. On the other hand I think she might fall apart when I die. She's stronger than she thinks though so she'll get over it. As will my parents, especially when Paul is born. I really do love them even though they probably don't think so. It's just time for me to be with mom. I don't know when I'm going to do it. I was considering tonight but I have too many obligations tomorrow. Emily would probably find me and that would just be a big mess. I feel bad doing this to her too but she's one of the strongest people I know so I know she'll get through this. I guess I'm a little scared. I wish I could take Cracker and my 'And the Band Played On' CD with me. They are perhaps my two favorite things in the world. Anyway this is probably going to be among my last entries. I apologize for boring whoever happens to be reading this. There was simply no one else to talk to. Love Electra

APRIL 7, 1999

Well it's all falling apart. I'm falling apart. It's not even the tangible stresses that are making me want to die. For the first time it's the depression itself. I have self-inflicted cuts all over my arm because hurting myself is the only thing that calms me down. I have to die Saturday at the latest. And I can't tell Kelly beforehand because she doesn't understand anymore. She's off in Brian's world. She complains about her guy problems all the time, and I understand that Pinekin treated her like sh——t and Perchanth ... well I think he was a little too deep for her. Not to say that she's shallow cause she's not, but this rage against Niecie is completely unfounded. Niecie is a smart beautiful girl who happens to like Perchanth. Kelly should get mad at him for their relationship not her. That catty craze is what allows men to rule the world. Anyway the writing is calming me down. I don't know why I've been so reluctant to start lately. Part of me just feels that it reflects my procrastination in terms of my impending suicide. I'm beyond the point where anyone can help me. It's just as well that my family has abandoned me. I was just bringing them down. I think that dream I had last night was really telling. I think my parents really do hate me, and losing another family is just not something I can deal with. I love them. God I love them, but all I ever do is hurt them. I deserve their hatred, but it still makes me so sad. Anyway my time on this planet is very short. I think I'll stick around to say one last goodbye to William who doesn't seem nearly so cute now that I know he's married. I just can't look at a married man that way. I guess that would have been a virtue had I lived long enough to exercise it. I hate this school. I love my friends. I love my parents. I hate my life. Why they feel the right to keep me here is beyond me. But I'm tired and so so sad and hurt. The sun doesn't shine for me anymore and that was what did it. When I really can't feel any pleasure at all. Maybe I'm being selfish but I don't think so. I think that, in the end, we all have to live for ourselves. We strive to support our families but even that is self-serving because we love them. I'm all alone in this world and I don't really know who I'm living for anymore so I'm through. And I'm sorry it had to end this way. I really wanted to be a mom but I just don't have the strength to hang in there any longer. Besides, I miss my mom. I want to be with her. She's the only one who ever loved me just because. She'd be sad to see me here sitting here a pathetic husk of my former self. I couldn't even tell her how this happened. I'd just have to hang my head down like I do in front of my parents. But unlike them she'd hug me in return. Love Electra

APRIL 8, 1999

Pondering (when I should be sleeping) my imminent departure and this new practice of cutting myself to calm my nerves. I wonder if anyone has noticed my arms. I don't dare wear short sleeves but I often roll up my long ones without thinking about it. If Kelly ever saw this she'd freak out. On the upside I think my death will provide a wake up call to her parents. My friends have been unknowingly asking me about a future that doesn't exist and parents who might as well not. I wonder if they know that they're seeing a ghost. It was over from the time I finally resolved to die. Parts of me are already dying inside it's just a matter of destroying what's left of the glue that binds them. I'd like to say goodbye in person but no one will accept that except maybe Betsy. I haven't decided whether I'm going to write her or not. I feel that I probably should because she's been the only one with an open mind during this whole mess. I love her dearly and I'm going to miss her terribly. Anyway, I'm getting sleepy so I'm going to try to go to bed without disturbing my wounded arm. It's funny enough that I felt like I'd never go to sleep before I added the new marks, go figure. Love Electra

APRIL 10, 1999

In about 48 hours I'll be dead. Sunday/Monday I'm going to die. No questions asked, no more putting it off. My arm is beyond the point where I could actually explain it and sound like a sane rational person. It's a mess but I still think it's pretty sad. I was going to show Kelly earlier in its progression but I never got the chance. I feel really bad not saying a proper goodbye to William. My intention was to show him that it was over and I think I did that. I don't want him to feel that he failed me in anyway because it's completely not his fault. I was beyond saving from birth. I can't wait to see mom. I really hope I end up getting to be near her for a while. I hope my death doesn't scare my cousins or my aunts and uncles for that matter. I figure now is a good time to go because there's so much other stuff going on that they probably won't have a whole lot of time to worry about me. I guess some concerned relatives might call tomorrow but I won't be calling them back. What I need right now is silence. I'll have fun with Randy tomorrow night but aside from my friends I really can't worry about anything anymore. My family is strong. It will take care of itself. What I'm looking for, and heading towards is peace. Sure there are lots of reasons for living but they all require more strength than one lonely depressed neurotic teenager can muster. At 19 I'm just so tired and so sad that none of those reasons seems good enough for staying. God knows I feel guilty about leaving but living a life filled with loneliness and self-hatred is not something anyone should have to live with. I miss my dad. He was so big and strong. I always felt safe around him. I could always hug him just because. He wasn't perfect but he wasn't a terrible father when he was around. And I was his. I love you Daddy, wherever you are. Love Electra

APRIL 11, 1999

Well Aunt Deborah has joined the cavalry. Any chance I had at getting a little breathing room during my final hours is gone. Anyway, I won't be speaking to her again. I can't deal with being patronized by anyone right now. My arm is bleeding away as it does every night. It is morbidly fascinating. I guess they'll have lots of fun analyzing this in the coroner's office. I'm debating sticking around until after my next meeting with William. I feel this intense need to fill him in on my accident theory. But I don't know if I can hold Aunt Deborah at bay for that long. I don't want her flipping out and showing up in Philly while I'm still alive. At the same time Mondays generally aren't bad for me and I should probably say a proper goodbye to William although he won't know it when he hears it. It's a tough decision. But that aptly timed fortune cookie said not to be hasty, and I am inclined to listen to it and maybe put it off two more days. I'll tell Aunt Deborah I have to sub for someone at work. I love her, but I can't deal with her right now. Actually, the rest of the family is bound to come calling soon too so I might need to hurry it up. Yeah I'll send William this email and then I'm out of here. There's really nothing left for me here. I'm feeling especially bitter tonight because I feel like the whole world, with a few exceptions, has turned against me. Aunt Deborah was the one hold out because she didn't know any better but in the end she is gone too. In a way her joining the familial brigade has given me the freedom to leave without as much guilt. They don't understand what I'm going through on any level where they could possibly be of assistance. And so here I am completely alone, but at peace with the idea of my leaving. Except for William and Kelly, more or less there's nothing left to say. I'm not even sure I'm going to leave a note. It seems like I'd only be repeating myself. But I guess I owe them at least that. Love Electra

APRIL 12, 1999

I just got a new lease on death from Aunt Deborah. Yep it's official, my parents hate me. On the one hand I should get myself over with, but Alicia has unknowingly inspired me to stick around for fling. I really don't want to ruin it for the suite so I think that I should stay. That also means applying for financial aid and writing my English paper, but certain sacrifices must be made. I don't know if I can hold on til fling but I'll try. I'm so tired of all this. Aunt Deborah unwittingly put the last bit of earth on my grave via the conversation we had tonight. I'm trying not to be mad at my parents for not understanding, but it's hard. Parents are not supposed to treat their children this way. Although I'm not their child they did pose as parents, at least for a little while. Anyway I've never been this happy about dying before, but suddenly I feel elated and free. I can't wait to see mom. I don't think my friends, for the most part, will be too shocked by my death. I think Kelly's expecting it soon. I'm sure William is too. I mustn't forget to make my list of reasons for living and dying. The former should be a long list of b.s., but if it will ease William's fears then I guess it's worth it. Hopefully, I'll be able to fully convey to him my accident theory. This life simply cannot be right. I started work on my suicide note tonight. It's coming out sounding a little bitter towards my parents and my family so I'll have to take a break and then rethink it. Anyway, I'm off to bed. It's raining, so I should sleep well. Love Electra

APRIL 14, 1999

A brief entry because the sun's almost up and I have to go to sleep. The crushing sadness came by today and spent about three hours giving me shaky hands and heartburn. It was a pretty solitary day. The milk I drank yesterday came back to haunt me. I told William everything I intended to and I would say that he understood (we're talking basic comprehension) maybe thirty percent of it and understood the impact of none of it. He's going to England next week, which makes my intended time of death all the more convenient. Modeling is really my last hope. I don't know why I've been putting off asking Tina about it. Another thing I've been putting off is calling my Aunt Jessica. I feel terrible about life under these circumstances. I don't know what to say to her. My parents hate me, that's already been established. I don't want to be alive anymore, well I certainly can't tell her that. And I still haven't managed to fess up to that math grade to anyone, and I know she'll be asking. And I don't want any guilt on her that maybe her conversation with me sparked my suicide. But I don't think it's right to avoid her for another five days. I think I'll call her when I'm pretty sure she won't be home. I know it's terrible but I can't talk to her. I can't talk to any of them ever again. It's too late for me. I'm already dead. In just five days that will really mean something. 'Til then I've got to keep going. It's like swimming in hardening cement. Love Electra

APRIL 15, 1999

I keep telling myself I'm going to bed at a decent hour, but I can never go through with it. I think maybe I'm afraid of the dark, but I'm not sure. Today is Dad's birthday. I just realized that his is exactly a month after mine. I still miss him, but I've given up any hopes of seeing him again. I wonder if my family will even tell him when I die and if so will he care? I should have gone to live with him after mom died. Father's can't give you away. I have no energy for anything now. It's taken every ounce of my strength to at least give the appearance of being a functioning individual. Hopefully, fling will give me a temporary injection of life. Aunt Ellie sent me an email today, and I couldn't even finish reading it because I can't concentrate on anything that long. She still loves me. And I love her and her family too much to continue to burden her with my problems. I just hope that she'll be there for Aunt Deborah because I know this will be hardest on her. She's the only one who ever wanted me to belong to her, except Mom of course. But I couldn't be hers and grow and breathe. I hope she has a full and happy life without me, but I'm not sure she can. She should adopt a child. Hopefully I will have taught her that children need to be loved and free. Few parents get that, but I think the human race would be better off if they did. Mom understood that even if she didn't completely realize it. It's why, although she didn't always protect me from the elements or give me the best lifestyle for a child, my heart will always be hers. I could have been Uncle Phillip and Aunt Susan's but they didn't want it. So now here I sit arm scarred and bleeding with an unfounded terror in my throat. This is that same nightmarish feeling I had in all those train track dreams. They've finally come true. I wonder how my subconscious knew where I was heading all those years ago. Maybe this was inevitable. But I hope not. It makes me kind of sad to think I was doomed from birth. Love Electra

# Chapter 4

# Parents

APRIL 19, 1999

I almost came to tears today over my impending departure, which will take place sometime within the next 24 hours. I was thinking of Patricia in her little stretch pants that make her look so much like a miniature person. I pray to God that she leads a happy successful life, and I think she will. With parents as loving and devoted as hers she's got the best possible starting ground. Part of me hopes that she'll forget me. The more selfish part of me is heartbroken by the idea. I'm completely unsure of how I should say good-bye. There really is no appropriate way under the circumstances. I wanted to leave behind some touching moment for my loved ones to remember but that wouldn't even matter in the face of the legacy of debt and cowardice I'm leaving. I'm a little scared, but mainly I've made peace with my self. The what-if still plagues me though. What if I had been on Luvox (or rather something that works) when I came to Penn? Uncle Phillip never understood that the out of control spending was directly related to my depression. When material goods are the only things that even temporarily relieves your pain (at least that you have access to) it's very hard to give them up. I hate to think that a few more, or rather a lot more hugs and kisses from them, and an 'I love you' every now and then would have helped me live. I've crafted respite from the pain of this loneliness for four years now. It was never the CDs or the other junk I collected. I just wanted to belong. I think the tears are all in my heart now. Maybe that's why I can't cry. It feels like it's about to burst. I can't even stop to think about the lives I might destroy. I think Aunt Deborah will probably be the only one. That can't stop this though. I love her, but in the end she has always been more a part of the problem than the solution. Aunt Ellie is strong. She'll get over it. And Grandpa, well I really don't know how he'll handle it. I feel like they've all turned against me anyway, except for Aunt Ellie. The spoiled ingrate, my uncle, in the end, made money the most important or rather significant thing in my life. Not on purpose, of course, but he's so wrong to think that people don't need each other. We need to be strong individually, but love is the fuel behind that strength. I do not have the strength to wait around until someone comes to pull me out of this pit and love me just because. I wish I did because I can't stop hemming about the life that should have been. If only I'd been stronger. If only she had lived. Instead, I'm dying alone in my disgrace. And all I can say is I'm sorry. But then again, I wasn't worth the trouble in the first place. So I guess that, in the end, I'm doing them all a favor. Love Electra

APRIL 20, 1999

I am losing my mind. The fear is so intense, and I can't even directly attribute it to anything. Am I afraid of my own family? The bitchy patronizing message Aunt Deborah left on my answering machine didn't help my emotional state, but that inspired more anger than anything. I think it might actually be the Luvox. This is kind of how I felt on the Prozac, but taken to a new level. The nightmares are becoming more and more vivid. I've got to get out of this. I'm sick to my stomach and my head and chest are throbbing. The only reason I'm still alive is that I really want to finish 'NightShift.' What a sad reason to stay alive. Sometime in the next 24 hours though I know I keep saying that, but it's really going to happen this time, it has to. I hate to destroy God's creation but every now and then a defective product comes down any line and it's bound to break sooner than most. I wish I could say goodbye to William but I can't wait that long. Tonight after I wash my hair and shave I'll cuddle Cracker and take my departing breaths. I don't want to die angry at Aunt Deborah but I guess that can't be helped. In the end she is so different than any of the other aunts and uncles. I found my own strength in Aunt Ellie. It's too bad that I didn't realize how much I needed her until it was too late. Her guilt trip rings hollow because I know in my heart that I love my family. If I didn't it wouldn't hurt so much to leave them. Aunt Deborah's guilt trip rang hollow when I considered the fact that my grandparents have probably called me fewer times than I've called them since I've been here. All I hear is the 'everyone loves you and cares about you' from the two people who are actually speaking to me, but when it comes down to it even when I'm clearly about to break, my needs are not that important in anyone's eyes. I know it sounds selfish but it's true. I'm so scared and feel so alone. Why can't they forget the guilt trips and the past offenses? Why can't someone just love me? There comes a time when we need to put our lessons aside and just hug the pupil because lessons are hard to learn and we need to see when the student just doesn't have the strength. It requires a lack of self-interest I hardly ever see. Ironically enough my grandmother definitely has a little bit of that light. And so does Aunt Ellie. Mom had it toward me sometimes. It's raining. What a beautiful dawn. I'm glad that my last day is a wet one because I've always felt most at home in the water. Love Electra

APRIL 21, 1999

If all goes according to plan this will be my last entry. I debated over whether I should stay until after this weekend, but I think it's best that I go now. I feel like there are a million things I was supposed to do in preparation, but haven't gotten around to it. I've decided not to leave a note because I don't know what to say besides I'm sorry again. I feel like, since I'm choosing to die, I really don't have the right to say where my things go. I just want to be buried with Cracker that's all I ask. I was scared a little earlier but now I feel calm. I just stopped to take the antihistamines. I took five so I don't think they'll take long to kick in. I took them with milk though, so I'm hoping that I don't throw up. I wish that I had had the opportunity to say good-bye to Em and Kelly but how do you do that? My computer is shutting down for the last time. Hopefully they'll have mind-sweeper in the after life. I'll miss my friends and my family. I hope that my death doesn't inspire any guilt in any of them because this is all me. I got myself in this pressure cooker. I was wrong to assume that it would ever turn off. Well I have to do a few things before I fall asleep. I loved a lot of people, but in the end it was bad for them all. I hope they can find it in their hearts to forgive me. Love Electra

*These are not the words of a martyr. This is the anatomy of self-hatred that masquerades as self-confidence to the world. Electra refers to her aunt and uncle as her parents, but never to them as dad or mom. Yet, Electra rebuffed every attempt her aunt and uncle made to show love, parent, protect, and guide her. While appearing to go through normal teenage growing pains, what Electra endured reached well beyond natural teenage rebellion.*

*Her Uncle Phillip was always an affectionate person. During family gatherings, he readily extended hugs and kind words to all. But, whenever he tried to hug Electra, she would flinch and freeze as if paralyzed by fear. After her first hospitalization uncovered her memories of abuse, she revealed to her family how much she hated being touched. She put them on notice never to touch her, but their respect for these terms only served to further sabotage a nurturing relationship with her. The letter* from her uncle that she received on her nineteenth birthday, was a simple contract that he asked her to sign for the purpose of bringing financial stability to her life and preventing financial ruin to him and his wife. The contract outlined her budget for the school year; the uncle asked her to agree to the terms by signing her name, so that she would gain some sense of responsibility for keeping its terms. Her response was to project self-hatred onto the uncle thereby convincing herself that the contract was based on their hatred of her rather than their loving attempt to provide guidance as parents. Perhaps it was more the image of status that allowed Electra to boast having two professional people as parents to her college friends because, from the first day she moved in with the aunt and uncle, her rejection of them as parental figures was immediate and incessant.

Then again, what child doesn't rebel against parental efforts? The two-year-old who insists on pulling away from the parent's safety hand to run into traffic, the struggle to keep that hand while confronting the ensuing temper tantrum are motivated by the deeper desire for that child to stay alive. On their own, children refuse to take naps and fight parental efforts to regulate their sleep. Parents know that poor sleep regulation over time can make people sick both physically and emotionally so they insist the child go to bed and wake up during optimal, health-promoting hours. Then there are the universal "I want, I want" demands parents face, beginning with small toys and evolving into bigger, more expensive toys and clothes as the child grows. Unchecked, the child never learns the difference between "I want" and "I need" resulting in material self-indulgence that becomes incorporated into the growing child's need for loving nurturance. Love is limits. If the growing child is not taught limits, she never understands love or learns the life-sustaining elements of love.

Like playing in traffic, parents know how financial ruin destroys life and try to do what is necessary to hold firm to life-prolonging limits, just like holding the toddler's hand. In many ways, Electra never stopped having the temper outburst more openly triggered by the contract from her uncle. Unlike the two-year-old who eventually settles from the tears as she is made to trust the loving direction given, Electra did not settle and did not have enough internalized love to trust the guidance being offered.

Over time, her inability to trust her family became increasingly evident. For the aunt and uncle she called parents everyday living with their niece was like being devoured by an emotional suction cup. She was constantly asking them to buy things: new clothes, new shoes, name brand soap, jewelry, and technical equipment. In the morning her breakfast discussion was a list of things she wanted them to buy and in the evenings, another list. Whenever they questioned why she needed to replace clothes and other items so soon after the last purchase, she would become emotionally frazzled, as if about to cry, and seclude herself in her room; seemingly a typical teenage outburst, but, in fact, these were the times she wrote the most about *taking her own life. It is not an exaggeration to say that her purchasing demands were incessant as were her reactions when her demands were challenged. Though it may have seemed that way, Electra was not a spoiled child. The aunt and uncle felt like they were "walking on eggshells" around their niece, always expecting more moments of her purchasing demands and frazzled withdrawal when they did not do as she wanted. When she went away to college her spending worsened, as she collected credit cards and constantly called on her parents to help her pay them off.*

*She wrote about how she loved her Aunt Deborah the most, but what she didn't reveal is how she left her aunt in financial turmoil. Aunt Deborah had difficulty saying no to Electra and so showered her with the expensive restaurants and items that she couldn't afford. While her parents were trying to help her with life-sustaining guidance, her Aunt Deborah gave into her demands often undermining the parents' efforts. Electra writes about her aunt being weak, but she regularly exploited her aunt's weaknesses. Perhaps she was not cognizant of her exploitation. But the more obvious omission in her diary about her grades is something unlikely to be subconscious.*

*Even while her parents were helping to pay her tuition and other school fees not covered by her loans and scholarship money, Electra refused to share her college grades with her parents. When she was in the private high school, grades were reported to her parents who reviewed them with her and guided her into optimal performance. Both parents had advanced degrees and considerable experience with developing effective study habits. When they shared their experiences with Electra during high school, her grades improved dramatically. The guidance was good sense: regulate sleep, no TV in the bedroom where studies occurred, minimize distractions, develop healthy outlets like exercise or some hobby of interest. Electra's reaction to this guidance in high school was always to revisit taking her own life, always to escape life and thereby escape the direction she was being given. Albeit reluctantly, she did start an exercise program and the TV was removed from her room in her aunt and uncle's home. These interventions improved her academic performance and, in fact, helped her excel to the point of being a most desirable applicant at every Ivy League university in the country.*

*This slender, graceful beauty then went to college and made frequent calls home to her parents requesting money, refusing their advice and becoming increasingly frazzled when they refused her. The first thing she did when she started college was bought a TV and collection of video games for her bedroom. Against the advice of her aunt who explained to her how ineffective medication would become if she kept stopping it, Electra routinely stopped her antidepressant medication without telling anyone and replaced it with excessive amounts of Excedrin. Even though her parents had purchased a college meal plan for her, she rarely used it and, instead, ran up credit card and college account bills eating out in expensive restaurants. Given these conditions Electra designed in opposition to parental guidance, it was no surprise that her grades deteriorated. However, she always told her parents that her grades were fine and never did show them a grade report, even though they asked to see it many times. Unlike high school, college grade reports are only sent to the students, even though the parents are paying the bills. College advisors are bound by confidentiality when the student refuses to allow permission to share information with parents. By the end of her sophomore year, her meager academic performance resulted in the loss of part of her scholarship money. But her parents did not know why she had lost scholarship money. She did not tell them even while expecting them to make up for the lost money by paying more of her tuition.*

*Like the toddler fighting safe constraint, Electra wanted to be free to play in traffic. She reverenced the memory of her life as an autonomous child, with a mom and dad who she states loved her. She would rather die than have the autonomy shaped by her mom and dad challenged. But for reasons she may have understood near the end, she doesn't refer to her mom or dad as parents. That year, just before her ninth birthday when she told her mother about the sexual abuse she suffered while left alone during an adult all-night party, her mother decided that it might help Electra to have her spend more time with her father, Thomas. To the little girl Electra's surprise, her dad had been living only a train ride away in Manhattan with his wife and infant daughter at the time. It excited Electra to finally have the chance to get to know her real father after years of calling her grandfather "daddy." And so, from the age of nine until she was almost twelve, Electra was sent to spend weekends, summers, and some holidays with Thomas and his family.*

*Thomas's wife was kind to Electra and she became close to her half sister. But her father's motives for agreeing to these visitations, after nine years of refusing to acknowledge Electra's existence, became painfully clear to Electra's intelligent and sensitive soul. His words to her were always abrupt and cold. His demeanor was demanding and authoritarian. When Electra came to stay with him, Thomas would disappear with his wife and leave Electra to baby-sit her half sister. Conversation between Electra and her father was rare and when he did talk to her she found it painful. Electra's aunts and uncles begged her mother to stop sending her there, as it was increasingly evident that the father only wanted her around to baby-sit and free up his weekends so that he did not have to care for either daughter during vacations. During one of the family trips to the Midwest, Electra met, for the first and only time, her paternal grandfather, uncle, aunt and cousins. Whatever actually happened to Electra during this trip was serious enough for her mother to finally discontinue further visits between Electra and her father. She was a preadolescent, barely eleven, when she first began to contemplate taking her own life. Thomas was not heard from again even though Electra knew he still lived nearby in New York. The next and last time she saw her father was at her mother's funeral.*

*For most of the years that Electra lived outside of Baltimore with her aunt and uncle, her father was living less than an hours drive away also in Maryland. As a result of a job change, he had moved his wife and daughter from Manhattan to a Baltimore suburb. If he wanted to find his daughter, Electra, he knew how to contact her grandparents and easily could have found her. Electra knew this and longed to be found but had no idea that he was still as close as he was. These were the "mom and dad" she longed for in her diary, not to be confused with "parents."*

APRIL 22, 1999

I should be in bed but I'm not really tired. It seems like a waste to spend my few not-tired hours in bed, but on the other hand I do feel safest in bed, which is why I'm happy that I'm going to die there. You're probably wondering why I'm still alive. Well the most obvious reason is that the antihistamines didn't put me to sleep. On the contrary they kept me awake. So it looks like I'll be putting that off a few more days. I really don't want to go to the Poconos this weekend but if it's one last thing I can do for Stephan then I guess I should. Tuesday night should be my last. God that seems like an eternity but that's the most opportune time. I'm really worrying Sabrina because I avoid the phone and email like the plague. One more nasty message on my answering machine from my family and I'm heading over to the high-rises. Jumping out of one of those windows would be ideal, but it's a lot harder to set that up than suffocating in a plastic bag. I'm using the one I got from HUP because it's clear and I'm less likely to panic if I can see. The scars on my arm are finally fading. I've resisted the urge to make new marks because always wearing long sleeves is a pain in the but. Anyway, I guess there isn't a whole lot else to say. I'm almost done with 'Night Shift.' Bette Midler will be my new reason to live. Love Electra

APRIL 23, 1999

It's like being in a dream or rather a nightmare. Something out of a Stephen King novel, but definitely I've lost all concept of time, and things that used to hurt me like snide comments from Emily, don't bother me much anymore. Even the spider crawling up my wall didn't freak me out, well that much. On the other hand I'm in a constantly terrified state, literally afraid of my shadow. I thought about telling William this but I don't think he can do anything about it or wants to hear that sort of stuff. This is truly bizarre. While my friends experienced their second to last day of classes, I experienced the last Thursday of my life. It is now the dawn of the last Friday. It's an almost mind boggling concept, but at the same time, it's comforting. I am sad to think that there's no turning back. I mean even if the man of my dreams showed up could I fix my entirely screwed up life to a point where I could live? Anyway I don't communicate with anyone outside of Hill now. I sleep, work, eat, read and play computer games. I abhor email and am considering unplugging my phone. My parents forwarded my HUP bills without even looking at it. I don't understand how you can hate someone for being sick. I mean it's not like I was fine before the contract and fell apart just to spite them. I was falling apart before that ever happened. He chose to lay that on me when I was clearly not at my best and sure that was the straw that broke the camel's back, but I didn't choose to try to end my life solely because of it. The very idea is ludicrous. Even I valued my life more than that. He put the last nail in my coffin and led me to a point where I couldn't turn back. It's damn scary to be here, and I wish I could get it over with but I don't want to play the victim. I just don't see why I'm being made to feel like sh——t by these people who claim to love me. That my parents aren't even speaking to me says a lot. I know they don't love me now and now I wonder if they ever did. I stepped into my grave four years ago and, my God, what a mistake it was. I loved them wholeheartedly. I adored them. But it seems like I never went from legal burden to loved child. What a fool I was to think that they could ever love me that way. I just wish I could see Patricia and Raven again. I think I could die peacefully if I could but Patricia comes attached to people who hate me and I don't think Aunt Ellie would be thrilled to see me either right now, talk about conflicting emotions. I feel so guilty being so angry at my parents. I mean the failure that is my life is completely my fault. But on the other hand I wish that they had told me four years ago. Maybe then next Tuesday would just be another Tuesday as opposed to the last full day of my life. It's a shame I was ever born. At least Mom could have had some kind of happy life if I hadn't been born. In fact everyone I know would have been much better off never knowing me. It actually does seem best that I dispose of this vermin before it infects anyone else. I can't remember exactly when I started to hate myself but clearly it wasn't soon enough. Love Electra

APRIL 24, 1999

Dawn of my last Saturday and what a beautiful Saturday it is. There's a bird in the tree outside my window. My friends have made me feel especially beautiful these past few days dolling me up for my last dance. I still don't particularly want to go but again I owe it to Stephen. I owe them all something for disrupting their lives with my suicide attempt and again with my death. Since I won't be around to apologize for the latter I'm trying to be a good friend now. I'm not so scared just now but I'm starting to regret that I can't turn back. You can't turn back when you're done and I am essentially alone. My family would deny that before turning away. I'm starting to regret that my life is lost because on some level I think it was worth something. I just can't figure out what my purpose was. Maybe I came so that mom wouldn't feel so alone. I think that having a child or getting married to someone who really loves you are the only possible cures for what I've got. If only I had the strength to wait for them. Well it's too late now anyway. I'm more or less gone. It still makes me sad though. Love Electra

APRIL 26, 1999

The dawn of my last Monday, I had an interesting weekend. The Poconos were better than I expected from what I can remember which isn't a lot considering how plastered I got. I got into a hot tub built for two with about five other people, ate a cigarette and passed out in someone else's bed wearing a wet bathing suit. I got calls from all my aunts. I called Aunt Ellie back and lied through my teeth about too many things including where I was Saturday. I feel terrible lying to her because she deserves my honesty more than anyone else. But I couldn't exactly tell the truth. I suspect that she knows that something is very amiss. My parents have completely given up on me and it sucks because I didn't get caught trying to kill myself, I got caught after I had decided against it and got stuck in a psych ward orphaned once again. But maybe this proves the fundamental difference between being a legal guardian and being a parent. A parent may use tough love but doesn't just leave when they stop enjoying the ride. I love them still and if they weren't abandoning me, I would stay alive. That sounds awful but it's true. I don't blame them for anything but letting me in in the first place. If they had expressed the fact that they didn't want me my feelings would have been hurt but I don't think I'd be preparing for my death at 19. There's nothing stable in my life anymore. Every time I've really, really needed an ally Aunt Deborah hasn't been of much help, and I'm not her child so I have no right to expect that of her, but she's not my child either and I can't be her rock. Aunt Ellie is the balance. I love them all but she is the one who kept me feeling human and not completely alone in this world. I owe her so much and she will always own a piece of my heart. It tears me up inside to know that I've been kicked through death's door by my own stupidity because, for once, I actually want to live. But I can't. I'm still not afraid but there's more than a little regret in my heart now. At least I am comforted in the knowledge that my death will, in the end, benefit them all. I have to erase any anger from my heart because in the end, it was all my fault and besides I don't want to die bearing any ill will toward others. Love Electra

## APRIL 27, 1999

My last meeting with William is today. We would have three more if I were going to be around but alas, I cannot stay. The will to live has slowly crept back into my soul but it's too late. The door has closed for good and been locked several times. It's a sad place to be. I already feel detached from the world but I suspect that that is due to fatigue more than anything. I'm still not scared, just a bit uneasy. The one thing that comforts me is the thought of seeing mom again. I guess I never fully recovered from her death. I still miss her all the time. I still feel empty. But most of all I feel alone. So alone that I can't function because in my ocean all there is is pain and this is no way to live. I guess I should start thinking of a note but nothing I write is going to have much impact given the circumstances. Anyway I'm tired so I'm going to end this. I want to rage against the dying of my light but I've already lost the battle. Love Electra

## APRIL 28, 1999

I've been granted a brief stay on my impending execution. My OPIM test isn't until Friday and I'm still trying to figure out the best way to put myself to sleep. I'm experimenting with Tylenol allergy sinus nighttime but I think I should have just stuck with Excedrin pm. So now I'm sure of when I'm going. My newfound will to live is already fading but I still feel bad about abandoning my friends. My meeting with William went well. He's a really great therapist, much better than Dr. Vasa. I think that he sees how painfully hopeless my situation is. They gave me my one-month suicide assessment after the session. I lied through the whole thing. I didn't see how I could tell them the truth without being sent back to the psych ward at HUP. Never again, I say which is why this attempt must be perfectly orchestrated. If they catch me again they'll probably commit me. The idea of actually succeeding seems a little too good to be true but I'm staying hopeful. I finally wrote to Sabrina, as I should have done a few weeks ago. I wonder how she'll take my death. It's really not fair to her because she isn't even fully aware of the circumstances; she can't be expecting this. Anyway I've lost the ability to enjoy anything. I sit there playing computer games because they're the only thing I can concentrate on, but not enjoying them at all, just another sign that I need to be put out of my misery. Anyway, the thing stopping me now is not wanting to screw the people I work with by not showing up at a shift. So Thursday night would be the best time for me to go. Unfortunately, I have an appointment with William Friday afternoon so that would be cutting it a little close if it doesn't work. I really don't know what to do. Dying shouldn't be this hard. Anyway the sun is rising so I guess I should go to sleep. The bad dreams are becoming a serious problem but there's really nothing I can do about them. Love Electra

APRIL 29, 1999

Now is the hard time. I want to go but am not all sure if I should wait until Saturday night or do away with myself now. The Tylenol allergy sinus pm has proven very ineffective in terms of putting one to sleep. And I'm not expected at work until 10 pm tomorrow so I have time. But Em's got finals today and tomorrow and I don't want anything to stress her out. Of course this means taking the OPIM final but at least I won't be around to see my grade. My biggest problem with waiting until Saturday is that if I fail I'll only have a few opportunities to try again. Then again I don't plan on failing this time so I guess I shouldn't worry about it. The issue of the note is a bothersome one. I need to ask them to contact some people they probably wouldn't think to call, so there definitely has to be one. But I really don't know what to say aside from that. I'm too dead inside to evoke any deep emotions in my writing and I don't want to sound cold. I finally got back to email. I asked Sabrina if I could stay with her parents for part of the summer, which I guess just goes to show that I don't really want to die anymore. On the other hand the idea of the white light at the end of the tunnel seen in near death experiences finally came to me. I find the idea very comforting. Even if it's not true at least it's some notion of the afterlife attested to, this millennium. My big fear is that it will just be black on the other side. I associate light with people. The thought just renewed my hopes that I'll see mom there. Anyway, I guess I'll face William one last time. Not that I have any objections to that. I wonder why he didn't become a bona fide psychiatrist. He'd definitely be among the best. I have no idea how he'll handle my death. I wonder if Drs. feel guilty about stuff like that. Hopefully they know better but it's got to be tough. I almost inadvertently revealed the fact that I've been cutting my arms in our last session. It was pretty stupid of me to allude to it, especially while wearing short sleeves. But the scars are practically invisible and I managed to get off the topic before he could explore it any further. Anyway, I will approach my final days without fear. I'm even going to try to enjoy them. Love Electra

APRIL 30, 1999

Even I am surprised by my own apathy. How can I not care this much? I'd skip my OPIM final if I didn't have so many friends taking it with me who would freak out if I didn't show up. My arms are bleeding again for the first time in weeks. I stopped after three though so I can still wear short sleeves. It's a good thing that I'm not planning on being alive this summer because Sabrina's parents don't want me either. I don't blame them either. And if I actually did have some feasible summer plan, I might sucker myself into living. Anyway my last meeting with William is tomorrow. I don't know exactly how I'm going to BS my way through that one. I feel bad lying to him but I can't very well tell him the truth. Anyway, hopefully I've helped his research in some form. I am going to ask him about the nightmares though I'm sure that they're not within his field of expertise. Going to sleep has become a scary proposition. My dream symbols book has been a little helpful in explaining what some of them mean, but I just want to stop having them. Aside from making me feel terrible emotionally, they're disturbing my sleep schedule so I wake up tired no matter how long I sleep. Speaking of which, I should be getting to bed before dawn so that I don't fall asleep during the test. I guess I am ready to go. This is definitely the calm before the storm. Love Electra

MAY 1, 1999

I'm sitting here, hopefully about twenty-four hours away from my death with two thoughts running through my head. One, I'm losing my mind, and two, how did I become this loathsome creature. I keep thinking I see something flying around my room out of the corner of my eye, and if I look straight at something it looks like there are colorless cobwebs floating before my eyes. So in other words I'm starting to hallucinate and I would say that categorizes me as being a bona fide psycho, just one more reason to hate myself. I'm looking at my life and realizing how pathetic I am. No wonder my former parents don't want me anymore. It's been four years since mom died and I'm still grieving, and I was almost raped when I turned five, i.e. fourteen years ago, yet every year around my birthday I start having nightmares about it. I don't get over anything. Whoever said I was a strong, bright person was clearly completely wrong because I'm actually a stupid weakling. I'm not even sure that my intended suicide method is going to work. If it doesn't I don't know what I'll do. At that point I guess I'll just have to find someplace to jump. I think I thoroughly freaked out William with my arm cutting. At least he won't be surprised when I go. I still don't know what to write in my note. I'm still trying to figure out how I got here. All I really wanted from my parents was to be a part of their family: a few kisses good-night, and 'I love you' once in a while. I wanted them to like me and love me like I was theirs. It seemed natural enough to me, but I guess it's not. And it was stupid of me to keep hoping for that year after year. My uncle's contract was just the last straw. It was something he should have done when I was fif-teen or sixteen and living with them rather than now when I'm on my own. I don't need anymore phantom menaces. And even if he had chosen to go through with it this year, why on my birthday when I'm clearly battling depression? I just don't understand. This clearly wasn't out of love because if he loved me at all he wouldn't have ditched me after my suicide attempt. I guess I didn't deserve the things I asked of them but at the very least, I loved them with all my heart. And I don't hate them for hating me. Instead I hate me for making them hate me. This worthless life is definitely not worth living. Even if I could go on, I thrive on love and stability and there is a disastrous shortage of both of those in my life, so there's just no point. I'm sorry Aunt Ellie and William and Kelly and all the rest who want me to stay. I should have gotten rid of this garbage right after mom died. Instead I waited four useless years, caused much pain, and was a general burden to society. As punishment I'm losing my sanity, and my life is still going to end so there really was no point. God give me strength. Love Electra

MAY 2, 1999

What a predicament I'm in. It seems wrong to kill yourself on a Sunday so I'm putting it off again. I just keep making excuses because I've discov-ered just a little too late that I don't really want to die. But I've screwed myself over so there's no turning back now. I'm in too much debt, have no one to turn to, and don't have the energy to keep up the fight. The only thing keeping me from completely losing it is the thought of that light at the end of the tunnel. I've finally come to disagree with those that think that God sends those who commit suicide to hell. If you think about it, we end up dying for our sins and I think that's punishment enough. I'm still not really scared so much as I am unnerved and saddened by the idea that I'm going to die without having done so many things. But I have this, albeit ludicrous, notion that my death will, or might, help Aunt Susan's newborn child live. I'm responsible for all the problems she's been having so far, so maybe in exchange for my life God will spare his. I know it's ridiculous but it could happen. And then at least I will have contributed something worthwhile to my family. I do feel bad leaving Aunt Deborah like this. For all the times she's gotten on my last nerve, I could never doubt that she loves me and never tried to hurt me. Maybe if she had been strong enough to hear the whole sad story we could have helped each other a little more. I guess that was what stopped me from accepting her in any parental role. She lacked the strength that I always admired so much in mom. It was what made me respect mom as well as love her more than anything. I see it in Aunt Ellie too. Anyway it's time for me to go. There's no putting it off much longer. Love Electra

MAY 3, 1999

It is the dawn of a new Monday and I'm still here, and even I don't know why. Excedrin pm in hand and I somehow managed to run out of time. I need a fairly large number of hours between the time I do it and the time I'm expected at work and it just took me too long to get started. So I'm condemned to live another day after this one and see William one last time, which for once I'm not looking forward to because I don't want to discuss the issue of the scars on my arms or my imaginary summer plans any further. Thank God we didn't have that conversation about my arm a few weeks ago because if he had seen what it looked like then, or what it's starting to look like now, he definitely would have prescribed a stay at chez Doube. At the same time I would like to know what's behind this bizarre practice. Anyway, I was a real bitch to Emily today and I feel bad about it. I mean it does seem like her one purpose in her dealings with me is to make me feel like an idiot, but it's no excuse for my being mean. I really do think that being mean is up there with the seven deadly sins in terms of things you should not do under any circumstances. We're all guilty of it at some point but some people take it entirely too far. Well what else can I say besides I'm exhausted. I've failed again but it won't be too much longer. It can't wait much longer. Love Electra

MAY 4, 1999

I really wanted to go tonight. I mean for the first time in at least a week I had a serious yearn to die. Unfortunately the timing was off again so I couldn't. My meeting tomorrow promises to be awkward. But then again everything else tomorrow promises to be a little weird. If I die, great, but if not they will probably commit me. Aunt Jessica called me at 1:30 this morning. I was in the bathroom when she called so I didn't talk to her but I thought that was odd. Apparently the two or three members of my family who care are worried about me. I think they know that something's up. My suicide note sucks so I'm probably going to rewrite it tomorrow. God I hope William doesn't ask to see my arm. It's quickly heading to where it was the last time I stopped. I'll have to think about something unrelated but important to talk about tomorrow. I'll also definitely be wearing long sleeves no matter how hot it is. I've finally really run out of time. If I did go to Arlington I'd have to jump off her roof and I don't want to do that to her. I miss her. It would have been a great summer if I'd spent it with her. I complain about her a lot but the truth is that I feel the absolute worst for leaving her. Anyway I'd better sign off so that I can wake up for my appointment. Love Electra

MAY 5, 1999

Well this is it. I'm on my way. My hands are already shaking from all the Excedrin I took. There was a brief scare with the rubber band but everything is in order. I don't know if they'll be surprised or what because it's not like a whole lot has changed for the better. My note is written, poorly, but written just the same. How could anyone remotely passionate about writing kill themselves? Writing the note is so hard. I wonder if Sylvia Plath even left one. I'm feeling pretty numb right now. I'm not happy about dying. If I could take back the last year of my life I would in a heartbeat. But it's unfortunately too late to turn back. God help me if there's a fire drill. I wish I could see my family one last time, but I couldn't put Aunt Deborah through the pain of having me commit suicide while under her care. I feel bad enough doing it to my friends. At least Em and Alicia will already be done with their finals. I'm starting to have a slight ringing in my ears. I'm wondering if it's the meds or my losing my mind, probably a combination of the two. Well anyway it's getting hard to write so I'm going to end this entry. Thanks for listening. Love Electra

# CHAPTER 5
# Belonging

*N*ot belonging somewhere means not belonging anywhere. To plan and plot to take life is a lifelong absence from the joy of living. All the while Electra planned her demise, she was, on the surface, calm, sociable, and convincing in her serene, soft-spoken, sometimes childlike communication style, not that she talked much when she talked at all. She so wanted to belong somewhere, to someone, that she was quick to form close bonds with people she knew little about. She had known her suite mates for barely a month before she referred to them as best friends in conversation with family. Boys she barely knew she loved and she was torn when they did not reciprocate these feelings. Even the aunt and uncle she called parents were virtual strangers to her; prior to her decision to live with them, she had had little communications with her uncle and only met Aunt Susan once. This seemingly desperate attempt to belong to someone would be understandable had these been the only caring people in Electra's life. The truth is that her grandparents were constant parental figures throughout Electra's life, as was her Aunt Deborah and to a lesser but significant extent, Aunts Ellie and Jessica and Uncle David. After her mother's death, even though everyone in the family offered to have Electra come and live with them, she was insistent on choosing to live with the family she knew the least about, and who knew the least about her. And all the while she lived with these parents her sentiment for the grandparents who were always there for her, even for the grandfather whom she called daddy, always bordered on disdain and contempt. She modeled her mother's persona in this regard—the same persona that would take in a felon off the street while rejecting the parents that loved her. And so Electra did not learn how to recognize what she yearned for so much. She belonged to a loving extended family that coddled her throughout her life, yet she writes and tells her therapist about always feeling alone.

*Her identity took refuge in her belonging to things, as this is where her mother had taught her to place value. When Julie traveled, it was to make money; when she returned, she showered her daughter with expensive items but rarely provided reassurance Electra needed. As she summed up her life, it was her inordinate passion for a small fuzzy stuffed animal named Cracker that she most desired to be buried with. Money, gifts, expensive clothes, jewelry, nail polish, electronic devices; these things formed the basis of her identity. To restrict her access to them was to restrict her life. Without access to them, life was meaningless to her.*

*She reveals how much she likes William but, in therapy sessions, never told him about her financial problems and denied that she was ever emotionally abused. Even while obsessively planning her death, she repeatedly told William that she had no plan or intent to kill herself. William's clinical notes suggest that he thought he had come close to understanding Electra, to truly helping her. But he was no match for the convincing facade of this beautiful pretender.*

*As part of her posthospital care, she saw, William, a postdoctoral psychologist, twice a week on campus at a center for cognitive therapy. Her hospital and discharge diagnoses were listed as acute major depressive disorder, severe and recurrent (no psychotic features) and posttraumatic stress disorder as a result of her sexual abuse at age eight. By the end of her last therapy session she was given an additional diagnosis of early onset dysthymia or chronic depression that began in childhood. William completed a genealogy chart as a reality check for Electra to think through just how large her caring family was. Unfortunately, the chart included her father's side of the family where rejection was overt and only added to her pain.*

*At the conclusion of the therapy, William wrote:*

From the therapist's perspective, there were several positive outcomes. Ms. Binet was able to understand and use the problem-solving model in relation to conflict in her family. . . . From the client's perspective there were several positive outcomes. Ms. Binet stated at our last meeting that she had found the problem-focused intervention helpful in reducing her habitual problem avoidance and in improving the balance of health to unhealthy relationships in her support network. . . . In terms of the Beck Scale scores, Ms. Binet's depression and hopelessness at intake were in the severe range, and at discharge were ostensibly unchanged. Indeed her scores were stable over time, despite Ms. Binet's verbal report and changeable life circumstances. When I asked Ms. Binet about this, she said, "I have felt this way for as long as I can remember, it is more of a trait thing with me."

*Lying is a funny thing in how readily it becomes a difficult habit to break. Even though the fragility of her ego was still apparent in the testing the therapist performed each appointment, she was purposeful in delivering the opposite message to William. The truth is that she secretly persisted in the ultimate problem-avoidance maneuver to plan her death, had not made any of the summer plans she told William about and was convinced that she had no support network. During her hospitaliza-tion, she allowed the therapist to talk, by phone, to her Aunt Ellie, but refused his subsequent requests to involve family lest her massive deception be uncovered. The therapist wrote:*

*Throughout the months that I was seeing her she was taking Luvox, 150 mg/day, prescribed by her Aunt Ellie Preston, MD. I consulted with Ms. Binet's aunt, Dr. Preston, at the outset of our work, but Ms. Binet declined my request to consult with her at the conclusion of our work. During our work I advised Ms. Binet on several occasions to take-up a referral to a psy-chiatrist for pharmacotherapy. However, Ms. Binet stated that she did not wish to pursue the referral because of the impending end of the semester.*

*She knew that her proclivity to lie would be revealed if the therapist had talked to her Aunt Ellie again, as, at no time had the aunt ever prescribed medication for her. If this had been revealed then the alert would have been triggered as to her sui-cidal imminence resulting in countermeasures that she did not want. Revealing this would also have raised suspicion about another diagnosis that William did not men-tion in his work. Like every human being, Electra developed with her own unique way of viewing and interacting with the world. Human views and interactions are shaped by experiences, some better, some worse, some tragic. How human beings modify these views and interactions to progress or egress in life equate to unique per-sonality styles.*

*Many people will better understand Electra's personality style if explained in the context of common Hollywood drama: the soap opera beauty, who lives in flux, instigating discord and vacillating between relationships, holding menial jobs, yet always surrounded by abundance. When the soap opera beauty doesn't get what she wants and fails at attempts to manipulate and deceive, she strikes out and gets drunk or plots to kill herself. On television, these dramas are enticingly addictive to many viewers because there are rarely any consequences to the beautiful woman, who always recovers to begin another cycle of lies, love, and manipulation. The drama goes on endlessly except when the person behaving in this fashion is not an actress. Soap operas are a medley of psychopathology, primarily personality disorders. In real life, consequences do occur. Electra was also beautiful with self-esteem so fragile that she would lie, love and manipulate to protect it. People in specialty professions would label her character style as a narcissistic and borderline mix. Such a label is only useful if it helps to understand who Electra was and why she did what she did. She belonged to her lies: the ones deliberately stated and the ones that pierced her subconscious into the painful existence she found so intolerable.*

MAY 6, 1999

I couldn't fall asleep last night. In fact I didn't fall asleep until this morning, which led me to wonder if perhaps I wasn't meant to go this way. Well my answer came by certified mail: a letter from my former parents with contents terrible enough to warrant the message 'to be opened after final exams.' Any doubts have gone flying out of my mind. I'd rather die than read that letter. Who else has ever inspired that kind of fear in me? What was I thinking all those years ago? How could I have thought that my aunt, who didn't even come to my mother's funeral, would ever want to be a parent to me or that my uncle, who had to be talked into going to visit his dying sister, could ever love me like a daughter. These are completely self-contained people. The world around them could disappear and they would not care. In a way I envy that about them, but at the same time, caring about other people makes me feel at least slightly useful in the general scheme of things. Anyway, I'm trying again tonight. The Excedrin gave me a nasty case of the runs and is tearing up my stomach but certain sacrifices must be made. I wish that things had gone right last night. I don't want to die angry at them. The sight of that letter makes me mad for some reason. I just don't understand how such a smart and loving man can have absolutely no empathy or knowledge of human emotions. How can they tell me he loves me when it's so obvious that he doesn't? I am a responsibility. Something to be clothed and fed but never truly cared for. When I die I'm sure it will make him angry at me (how dare she be depressed) but in the end, he'll probably be happy to be free of me so I guess it will balance out. I'm sure that letter is just signed (or typed) 'Phillip' no love both literally and figuratively. What a fool I've been. I loved him more than anyone, I really did. And in the end, I wasted his time, failed him in every possible way and all I could do to repay him was take my own life. It's a high price but it's worth it. He may never have liked me but for three years I almost had a father so I'll always be in his debt. Love Electra

MAY 6, 1999

Still waiting for my deadly dose to kick in. I'm rather puzzled by my uncle's envelope. Why would he send a letter by certified mail? Well I guess I'll never know. This whole situation is making me ill. I think I'm fooling myself about the possible causes. It's completely my fault. I really should have killed myself right after mom died. No wonder Uncle Phillip hates me. I'm an ungrateful brat in addition to being an all around mental case. Now I'm getting sleepy (finally) hopefully this is my last entry but we'll see either way. Love Electra

MAY 6, 1999

I am a complete failure as a human being. Here I sit a sad filthy testament to why abortion should definitely be legal. The big trick is harder than I thought it would be. My whole family hates me. Except Aunt Deborah, of course, but she's probably getting there. If I'm not asleep by five o'clock I'm going head first out of the window. I keep varying between feeling extremely guilty and anxious and not caring one way or the other. Actually I do care if I live. I've lost everything: my family, my intellect, and soon my mind. I'm feeling quite angry at my uncle and that makes me hate myself even more. It's one thing for him to be hurt but this blatant hatred? I mean is he really arrogant enough to think that I'd try to kill myself just to get back at him? To think that I actually felt the absolute worst for doing that because, I didn't want to hurt him. Love Electra

MAY 7, 1999

So I opened the ominous note and it was as bad as expected. I should have read it a few days ago, I wouldn't be here if I had. I walked down Walnut Street earlier thinking about how much I loved my uncle and how I really wanted to make things right with him. Now just a few hours later I hate him. How dare he BS me into thinking that he saw me as being like a daughter. How could you do that? He didn't even try to make things right. He dumps some callus contract on me when I'm just starting treatment for depression, not to mention on my damn birthday, and then dumps me as soon as I crash. I'm not saying that I'm blameless in all this cause I'm not by any stretch of the imagination. Even my father wouldn't do that. And it's one thing to say that it might be better for me not to live with them, but to send me some pseudo legal document. What a jerk. You're not supposed to treat your family like that, ever. This is ridiculous. I'll miss Patricia but I never want to see him or Aunt Susan again. I really don't want to be alive anymore. And so it goes again. Everyone I trust to take any degree of care of me leaves me: my mom, my dad, now them. Mom couldn't help it. Dad didn't even pretend to care. But I've spent three years hoping and praying that they would love me as their own. I tried really hard. I hate him. I hate him for making me think he'd stick by me. I hate him for making me think that he loved me. But most of all, I hate him for making me love him so much that my heart is falling apart because of his rejection. A few hours later, I've written him a pretty scathing, well at least for me, email about all of it. I can't start over again. I can't trust anyone to be my rock and everyone needs one. I guess his is Aunt Susan. How could he just discard me like garbage? He lied every time he ever said that he loved me. On second thought that wasn't very often so I guess I should have known. I can't even remember the last time I heard those words from Aunt Susan. Death would be a great thing right now. And I'm going to do whatever I can to achieve this state before this summer is over. I've never hated him for being a jerk before but he has destroyed my faith in anyone to truly love me. I never want to see either of them again. They can throw my things away for all I care and they can take back those damn pearls. I don't want the car or the desk or the futon. No ties to them whatsoever. And now I am completely alone. If there's no one to share this life with I might as well end it as soon as possible. The burning hatred in my stomach tells me that in the end he won. He tainted my soul. Love Electra

MAY 12, 1999

For better or worse I've decided to give life the benefit of the doubt, at least temporarily. Aunt Deborah is having her hysterectomy tomorrow and the whole family is upset about that and other things. It seems that the whole family knows about my suicide attempt. I finally broke down and told Aunt Deborah. I've still resolved not to speak to my former parents ever again but surprisingly my family has been very understanding of the situation. It's not my intention to turn them against them but at least I'm not alone in thinking that he's a jerk. Apparently he responded to my email. Unfortunately for him I won't be able to read whatever foul thing he sent me at least until September. I think I was a little too apologetic. I don't want him fooling himself into thinking that he could have me back if he really wanted me. That simply is not true. I'll never trust him again. True, I'll suffer most for our downfall but he'll pay too. He won't be at my wedding, nor will he ever meet my children. That is assuming that I make it far enough to get married and have kids. I'm really uncertain about all of this. Anyway, I am doing research into the possibilities. If I go, I'm going to do my best to make it look like an accident, for Aunt Deborah's sake. I'm thinking of giving myself a fatal case of hypokalemia. It all depends on how the next few weeks go. My uncle's going to stop by my Aunt Ellie's tomorrow. Being in the same state with him makes me uncomfortable but I guess it will be okay. I get the feeling that Aunt Ellie is angry at me. She doesn't seem to want to see or talk to me. I think she probably feels caught in the middle here. For a while I was too. Caught between self-preservation and the fact that I loved him more than almost anything. Our relationship was bad for me but I still miss it. The hatred is fading and at least it has stopped gnawing. But this is no way from being over. I wish it was but I get the feeling that I'll be explaining this a few more times in the near future. Just as long as my uncle knows I wasn't trying to hurt or manipulate him I'm relatively happy with my family's perspectives. Most of all I just wish that they missed me like I miss them. Fat chance, they're probably waiting impatiently for me to clear my stuff out. Love Electra

MAY 14, 1999

I guess William's brief assertiveness training has paid off somewhat. I had a most unpleasant conversation with my grandfather about the situation with Uncle Phillip. Naturally he took Uncle Phillip's side because he can't see how any child could dare disagree with the instructions of their parents. I think his newfound power over Grandma and Aunt Deborah has gone to his head because even he used to be more understanding. I was vague but honest, if that makes any sense at all. But at least I did manage to stick up for myself. I felt no fear. In fact I felt little severe mental anguish over the last few days, just this dreamlike numbness. Except for seeing my jerk of an uncle at the hospital nothing has really fazed me too much. This having the apartment to myself has made me feel almost human. That's going to end soon enough. I've come to the conclusion that I do still really want to die. Aunt Deborah so desperately wants to keep me here though. Telling her about the second attempt was a mistake, as I probably knew it would be. She's acting like a paranoid idiot about the whole thing. My Dad did call me back and she didn't tell me. The anger over that is just starting to sink in. I don't know if getting in touch with him, given my limited time on earth, is worth it or even fair to him. I'm sure he's going along just fine without me but is also probably wondering what's up. I've been such a coward. I should have ended this weeks ago but I kept chickening out; even Aunt Ellie's sick of me. The fact that Aunt Deborah expects me to live for her, kind of pisses me off, for obvious reasons. My health is rather shaky anyway. My hands are shaking so badly now and I feel so weak. Something's definitely not right. But no one else knows, and I don't care so nothing will be done. A healthy dose of potassium will put an end to this all. It should come any day now. Love Electra

MAY 16, 1999

Uncle Phillip sent me an email I have not yet received. What in God's name could he possibly have to say in response to my letter? Hopefully there's an 'I don't hate you' somewhere in there, but the statement would be pretty hollow coming from him. What else was that letter meant to indicate:

we love you so much we're disowning you? Anyway I'm still figuring out exactly what I needed from him so I'm sure he hasn't got a clue. On the upside I've discovered that this building actually has eight stories which gives me a definite way out once Aunt Deborah heals. I still haven't checked to see whether or not the roof is locked but if it is I know it will be open on July 4th. It would be poetically just if I died on the 14th but I might have to seize the opportunity on the 4th. Anyway I'm already starting to be a bit irritated with my patient, but I'm trying hard not to be. I definitely wasn't cut out to be a nurse or a niece. Mom was the only person whose over mushing I could appreciate. Love Electra

MAY 18, 1999

I'm at an unfortunate crossroads in my life completely unsure of what I should do. I can't go back to Penn, or at least not in September. I see no future but I'm still plagued by this enormous desire to have children. And who is this beautiful guy I keep dreaming about and how long can God possibly expect me to wait for him? I have this incredibly strong feeling that modeling is an answer. It would at least buy me some time. I just don't know what to do. The anger is hanging around today. I walked into Giant infuriated and then had a bona fide panic attack in the store. That was unpleasant but what it symbolizes is worse. I'm really losing my mind. I can deal with unhappiness but insanity is not an option. Aunt Deborah already treats me like a two year old in a psych ward. She's driving me nuts but I shouldn't complain because she's the only one that separates me from being totally alone in this world. I don't know where I stand with Aunt Ellie. I think she, like my ex-parents, has finally just gotten tired of me. She held out a little longer than they did so I shouldn't bitch about that either. I love all my aunts and uncles but I know that they would be better off without me. I think that's something people usually say to evoke pity but in my case it's true. I haven't investigated the roof just yet but I'm becoming more and more convinced that it's the only way out of this mess. Forget about staying for a future that may never be. Part of me really wants these dreams to be pre-telling, in fact all of me does. I'd love to wait it out but I don't have the energy. I'm in the severe stays of depression and starting to feel some manic impulses. God help me, and my family. Love Electra

MAY 19, 1999

I don't know how I could have even thought that I could go on in my normal state after this latest rejection. I've been rejected before by people I've life. But I haven't really. He shall continue to haunt me at least until he's in Florida. I miss Patricia so much but my hatred for her father outweighs my desire to keep her near me. I know I'm a typical spec of family gossip, but I feel that he's lost his right to offer anyone advice regarding me. I don't feel like I should be subjected to his crap anymore. He decided to terminate our relationship not I, so he needs to excommunicate himself from my life. Making my life miserable from afar is low even for him. Anyway, the uncertainty is ever present. I've had a surprisingly good day emotionally but my nerves have been especially terrible. I located the ideal jump off point on the roof. It looks like that might be the way this story ends. Something's got to give and it looks like I'm it. I can't sustain an angry heart for too long but I can stay hurt indefinitely. Love Electra

MAY 27, 1999

I'm at a weird point. Apparently Aunt Susan doesn't hate me and actually misses me (although Aunt Deborah might have just said that to make me feel better). Also, apparently Uncle Phillip is being a bigger jerk than he normally is because of the current chaos in his life. And apparently he (claims that) he wouldn't have cut me off if I had just not refused to sign the contract. So I guess that in his mind this is all my fault. Well I say how the f——k was I supposed to know that? And screw him anyway. On the upside the rest of my family excluding Grandpa, of course, agrees that he is being a jerk. But they are nonetheless furious at me for attempting to take my life (from them that is). So I got the usual 'Do you know how that would hurt me' bullsh——t from Aunt Deborah. If only she knew how much pain that guilt caused me beforehand in addition to the rest. Personally I think anyone whose first reaction to a suicide attempt is anger is about as selfish and unempathic as can be. Unfortunately they abound. I don't need any self-serving 'you don't have the right' crap. I need overwhelming positive reasons not to die. We shall see where I go from here. Today is Mom's birthday. She'd be a beautiful 38. God I miss her. I feel like the pain of losing her has taken over my life. I still can't function without her. She was the only essential player in my life. I could have lived without anyone else. I guess it doesn't matter now. I feel she was wasted on me but she will never stop being loved. Happy Birthday Mom. Love Electra

MAY 28, 1999

Their baby was born on the 27th a month premature but healthy. Funny, how one of the saddest days of my life, is one of the happiest in theirs. He wins again. He always wins. It's kind of strange to think of this cousin of mine who I'll probably never meet. Am I always going to lose? That's the question that my life depends on. Because if I am then what's the point of my sticking around for the continuation of this tragedy. Aunt Deborah gave me the God always makes a way speech, and she doesn't know how phony that sounds right now. That's what makes this time so frighteningly dire. I've lost my way. He goes on with his happy life but he has thoroughly destroyed mine, and an essential part of me in the process. I've relied on my ability to look to the future and see a path. It's not fair. I know it sounds whiny but it's true. Why do people who are mean have no problem stomping on others to get ahead? Why do they get all the rewards? He claims to be a Christian, but he only uses it when it suits him. Why does God listen to his requests with open ears and close his ears to mine and my mother's and Aunt Deborah's? Why doesn't being a nice person count for anything in this world? And why doesn't anyone care enough about me to understand why I'd do anything to end this pain? I just want one person to make me feel whole again, to love me without controlling me and to stand by me when I fall. They say that everyone has a certain amount of pain in their lives, but the degree definitely varies. I have to wonder why William was the only one who could see that. I don't want to get in a habit of feeling sorry for myself, but it seems like everyone is happier than I am or is more equipped to deal with their pains. For me the immediate future seems insurmountable. I've lost my life preserver after falling in the middle of the Pacific and no matter how hard I try in this, I'll either be rescued or drowned. I don't think anyone knows how close I am to drowning now. And they'd all be horrified to hear that at this point I welcome the prospect, anything to end this pain. It's manifesting itself physically now. This cannot go on much longer. Love Electra

MAY 29, 1999

The path is starting to reemerge, painful as it appears to be, thanks to Aunt Jessica. On this my Uncle's birthday, a birthday that I, sadly enough, couldn't care less about, I can finally lay claim to a glimmer of hope. My family is more or less on my side of this issue, even Grandpa. And it's not just their support that matters so much, it's the fact that they're allowing me not to feel terrible for being so angry at him. I'm still left wondering how this situation could possibly resolve itself. I honestly don't love him anymore and without that love I really have no good reason for associating with him. He's not a nice person. I don't want to be around him so I will gladly let him fade from my life. Unfortunately that means losing an aunt and two cousins.

## CHAPTER 6

# Rage Within: Depression's Fifth Dimension

JUNE 7, 1999

Phillip is an arrogant moron when it comes to dealing with people. He thinks that both suicide attempts were made in order to manipulate him. That makes me furious. What kind of person thinks that someone would subject themselves to a week in a psych ward just to get back at them? Give me a break. If anything I didn't go through with it because of him. And I hate him for that. I lived to prevent myself from hurting him and he makes my life miserable in return. It's not like I tried to get caught. If it were up to me he never would have known about it. I hate him right now more than I ever have. He's a pompous a——hole. I truly hope that I never have any occasion to speak to him again. I'm through letting him abuse my heart. For someone who has caused so much pain he's a real baby when it comes to taking it. I'm sorry, I can appreciate the fact that he supported me financially for three years, but he has taken a lot in return. I might lose my life and a whole future because of his cruel arrogance. The physical toll has yet to be seen. Even if I do survive I might never have children. Six months ago I wouldn't have thought twice before giving my life to save that man. But no more, you can only push even the most passive person so far. Worst of all I don't know if I can live with this. This is eating me alive. How do you get over being abandoned at your lowest point by a parent? He is the worst in a long line of men who have left incredible scars on my heart. He's worse than either of my attackers because I trusted him and he violated my life. I don't want to live an angry distrustful life. But I do want to live. I wouldn't have spent so much time pouring over my pain with William if I didn't. I could never fully or ever majorly attribute my past suicide attempts to him but if it comes to that again it will be because of him. Because he told me in no uncertain terms that I am not worth fighting for. I don't know if this can ever end for me. I don't know if I can ever be the same. Love Electra

JUNE 9, 1999

I've absolved myself of the crime, which my uncle has tried and hanged me for in absentia. It took a serious bit of thought. I had to put aside my rage and actually try myself. I've come to the conclusion that my uncle is wrong. I never thought he had enough heart to be manipulated. He never seemed to empathize or feel my pains in the least. And that's what it took, this attempt and all the ones known and unknown before it. He never seemed upset by my depression and, until a few months ago, it never occurred to me that he would be even temporarily devastated to lose me. The attempt in March was the hardest one before or after then. It was the first time I considered living permanently so as not to hurt someone, at least since mom died. And I've come to the stark realization that the reason I don't take my suicide attempts to be so disturbing is because I know that death for me has long been just and alternative not something to be dreaded or feared, just another option. I'm always on this balancing scale. Sometimes it tips in favor of life, sometimes death. What Phillip did was tip the scales a bit too far in favor of death. It was not death for revenge or death to manipulate because I could no longer handle life. We lose things all the time. Losing me would be just another loss. Aunt Deborah is wrong. I don't float in the center of our family. I bounce around. I'm easily forgotten when I'm okay. It's only when I'm in trouble that I become center material and that goes for everyone in our family. My family thinks that they've done a wonderful job showing me how essential I am by making me feel like sh——t for trying to escape my pain, but Phillip told the truth. When I am too much trouble I can be tossed away like trash. It's happened too many times to be denied. But if I choose not to stick around until I've floated into oblivion then that's my prerogative. I empathize with my family but I don't belong anywhere and no one has had to live this life but me so I cannot base my decision on anyone else. The scales are swaying wildly now. Where they'll rest I don't know for sure but Phillip's fingers are still resting on the side of death. Love Electra

*This life testimony from the heart, what amounts to the longest suicide note on record, speaks to the many aspects of a common experience called depression. A symptom that most people complain about at some time in life, depression is experienced as often as the common headache. Less universal as an experience is when this symptom becomes bound to other symptoms such as poor sleep, erratic appetite, poor*

need: to see a shrink, to collect some good memories, to have a relatively low stress summer? But I got none of it. So I'm still stressed and in pain. I still can't bring myself to come out of hiding and still don't know whom to put any faith in. The pit issue was important. I function a lot better when I have something to take care of. Ideally I'd have a cat but I would have settled for a ferret or even a hamster. I guess I need something to just let me give. I think that's why I love babies so much. They ask for nothing but you give them so much. I don't feel like I'm ever going to be able to function with all the pressures people face. I don't know how I'd respond to normal life because I've never had one. I don't know who I can be. From what I've seen I'm not missing much not being able to see. I think I understand people pretty well but I don't think I have many qualities. If solely on a practical level I think I'd be better off dead. You see this still has no foreseeable ending and that is simply unacceptable. I think I've taken enough crap not to deserve that. So what is there to do? Do I stay and take it indefinitely? Or do I keep praying for death as I do nightly. None of it seems to do any good and I can't answer the question. No more, I say, but how? Love Electra

AUGUST 31, 1999

So here is what it comes down to. Grandpa thinks the crisis is my fault. But he still loves me. So in effect nothing has changed with him. I am also not allowed to choose my own religion. I guess I knew that but it has just been reinforced. I am once again not having my period, which is leading me to question my ability to have children. So the point of all this is that I really don't have anything going for me right now. So what is my inspiration to stay on this God forsaken planet? The answer, I have none except guilt. I am thoroughly miserable but I can't leave because it would crush a family that clearly doesn't give a rat's ass about my feelings. If they did, if they looked realistically at my life, they would understand why I have to go. Phillip has managed to convince them that he was protecting his family, from what, big, bad me? So if I'm such a threat why not let me die? I can't do it anymore. I'm not smart enough to make up for the depression. I'm not pretty enough to make up for the timidity. I don't want to be here anymore. I don't think there's anything for me. Everybody leaves me or hurts me or both. Why am I under this obligation to stay for the use of the masses? To be bound and yet so disliked. I just want to get through college and get away. No more guilt trips. No more unwanted dependents. If I could just make it through these next few years maybe I could be okay. But maybe not, and that's the scary part. This might just be the beginning of a truly miserable existence.

I don't want to live like this. Please let me go, please let me go. I just want to be with someone who loves me unconditionally and brings me some peace of mind. But it may be too much to ask so just let me go. I don't want to bear the responsibility for breaking their hearts but even this small being doesn't deserve this. Love Electra bed. I so don't want to live. Why wouldn't god leave Eunice and take me? Why does he insist on punishing us? Love Electra

JUNE 25, 2000

I think Aunt Jessica suspects something. Every time she hugs me she seems like she's expecting it to be the last time she'll ever see me. Maybe she knows how severe the damage was more than the others. Aunt D isn't help-ing things. Her pushiness is just making the walls close in a little faster. I don't know what I'm going to do, and despite the size of my family, I don't really have anyone to turn to for help. Aunt Jessica is too far away and too busy. Aunt Ellie doesn't like me. Uncle David has his own children to deal with and aunt D is too, shall we say, imbalanced and moody. I started to lose it towards the end of the semester but my friends unknowingly helped me keep it together. Without them I don't know if I can make it. It's a terrible position to be in. Now that I have the means to do this, my life has just got-ten a whole lot scarier. If something should arise again to push me over the edge then there'll be no third stay in the psych ward, just a funeral. I am no longer protected by my own ineptness in the act of suicide. I'm not sure of whether or not I'm okay with that. I just need someone to sweep me off my feet and out of my misery. Love Electra

JUNE 27, 2000

Just a quick note on my continuing decline, which goes on for reasons not completely known to me: my mood has been shifting every five seconds or so. It's unnerving to say the least. The one bright spot in my life, which is the hope of getting a new computer in the near future, is probably a false hope. None of this seems worth it. I so thoroughly hate my job that I'd like to die just to escape that aspect of my life. Where does it end? People always dismiss the problems of the young thinking us too imbalanced or stupid to be able to differentiate between major and minor problems. And that does explain a lot of my history with my family. But these are not small gripes being overblown by a spoiled twenty-year old. These are changes that are slowly but surely halting my progress in life. If this continues as it has for so many years, the inevitable outcome will be my being unable to function at which point I will either have to die or be committed. Love Electra

JULY 8, 2000

I am turning into a monster. I've lost all self-respect and dignity. There is only despair. If I could find a quiet haven to think and not be bullied for just a little while maybe I could pull through. But instead I am cracking, publicly and especially privately. And there is no one here I can ask for help. Is this how it should end, with me jumping out of my bedroom window? Aunt D expects me to be there for Grandpa when I can barely hold myself together. I am at the breaking point. I'm so useless, especially concerning my grandparents. I can't bare watching Grandma deteriorate. She'll curl up just like mom did, but I'm not sure of how long it will take her to get there. I can't watch her die. One relative was enough. Aunt D is a very big stress in my life. She's determined to take away any autonomy I once had in life. But I've got no place else to go. I feel terrible about the impact my death would have on her and the rest of the family but I can't see it being avoidable in the relatively near future. I've come to realize that Aunt D and the others don't care at all about my feelings. I mean not at all. And they wonder why I'd want to leave. Love Electra

JUNE 9, 2000

When my new computer arrives I'll start working on my novel. This is in some ways my best chance to live. If I fail at writing then I'll truly have nothing to live for. It may seem silly to rest something so important on something so unstable but everyone needs to be good at something, and so far I've proven myself completely useless. Even Aunt D is getting tired of me. I don't blame her but I really don't know what I'd do if she kicked me out. Actually I do know but it wouldn't be good. This could've been God's intention when he created me. I've been in limbo for so long, and it's terrible. I so wish that I could see myself in a year or two just to know if I'm even worth fighting for. The way things are looking and feeling right now I doubt that I am, especially if there's no way out of this depression. I am so frustratingly useless. I've lost all control of my life and there's nothing to be done about it. I could quit school, get a job and move away but my head's not together enough and the family would go from disliking me to outright hating me. They want me to be there for Grandpa who also doesn't like me and also doesn't need me when I'm falling apart at the seams. I simply can't do it. That situation with Grandma is another nightmare in itself. I think she'll be better off dead than the way she is now. I can deeply sympathize with her plight. She has no control over her life and it's terrible. There's no telling how long this will go on. I just want her to come back, but she's just as gone as mom is. It's all breaking my heart. I can't watch this anymore or I'll crack. But for some reason I have to. I miss mom and grandma so much. I've run out of backers. I'm all alone, and I'm not strong enough to deal with it. All I'm doing is begging God to give me a reason to live. Love Electra

JULY 10, 2000

I am starting to worry people, mainly Aunt D, with my constant bouts of unhappiness. I don't want her input on the situation because it always proves frustratingly unhelpful. It's going to require more effort than I think I can muster to quell her fears. I understand how afraid she is of losing me, but it is quickly becoming a non-issue. I simply cannot stay this way. I wish my death could accomplish something like bringing Grandma back. But it seems destined to be as pointless as my life. Sadly enough I don't really want to die, I just really don't want to live. If I could see a light at the end of the tunnel, I would stay, but I don't so I can't. How did we get this far off course? I guess the depression makes me more hopeless than anything else does. I don't want to spend a lifetime on antidepressants, seeing therapists. I just want to be normal. But the events with Phillip have pretty much assured me that I will never really be normal. It was time for me to go five years ago, but I was a coward and now I'm suffering the consequences of my coward-ice. It makes me so sad to think of what might have been. If only she hadn't died. If only I hadn't chosen to live with Phillip and Susan, so many ifs that really don't matter anymore. None of this does, to anyone. Love Electra

JULY 30, 2000

These are the reasons why I'm afraid. I am unhappy for apparently no reason too much of the time. I am going at this whole college thing without a hand to hold. And I'm losing any will to live. Day by day I just wish more and more to be free of this place. I don't know if I'll be able to pay my tuition. It's worrisome to say the least. It's making me sick to my stomach and my hands are shaking more than usual. I wish that I dealt with stress like normal people. I'm tired of being so scared all the time, scared and lonely. I should just jump and get it over with. It surprises me that no one has figured out that I have a stress disorder. It's destroying me. Or maybe it already has. All I can do is beg God to make me better. I know that He can but I'm not sure if he cares enough to shine a little on this heart. This is getting very bad. Love Electra

AUGUST 1, 2000

I'm too anxious to sleep. The near future is becoming very uncertain. I'm so close to jumping it's scary. I feel terrible about what it would do to Aunt D. But what else can I do? I'm miserable and it's not fair. But more than that I don't know if things will ever get better. It would be different if there were just one event I have to get past but this roadblock is stretching into eternity. I know Aunt D and Uncle David and Grandpa all love me. I'm afraid that eventually they'll stop loving me just like Phillip and Susan and Aunt Ellie did. Aunt Jessica would be such an invaluable resource if only she were here. She loves me and she understands. But I can't ask her to put her life on hold and come fix whatever's wrong with me. I don't want to hurt anyone but I just can't stay. I hate to admit it even to myself but that business with Phillip really was the end for me. I can't trust people now. People get tired of me and they don't tell me until it's too late to make things okay. He lost me. I lost. And now I'm at a terrible crossroads with nowhere to go. Neither route looks like a good idea but I have to choose because that's just the way life is. Love Electra

AUGUST 12, 2000

It's been too long since I've written. I have a lot to tell you and no desire to tell it. Seymour is very sick but thankfully getting better. I don't think I've prayed so fervently since Mom was sick. Anyway, I've come to find out that Aunt D. is falling apart too. She poured her soul out to me yesterday making a bad day so much worse. I worry about her a lot. I'm pretty sure that she would commit suicide if I did which puts me in an awkward position. On the one hand I don't want to force her to live if she wants to go, on the other hand, I don't want to be the cause of her going. The family dislikes me enough as it is. As usual I don't know what to do. I just want to get married and have children. But I don't think I'm smart or pretty enough to attract a husband. No one wants a screwed up dim wit. I've tried to stop looking so hard though because my faith in God far exceeds my faith in myself. It's rough. I don't know how long I should wait before I give up hope and take the plunge. I spoke to Aunt Ellie today and it made me very happy, but there isn't much of that these days. I really miss Aunt Jessica. If she had the time and the proximity I'm sure she could save me. Well at least I have Seymour. Love Electra

AUGUST 13, 2000

It's been a terribly unproductive day. I couldn't bring myself to write more than a paragraph of the novel, much less than I'd hoped for. I don't know why I've been in such a fog today. I still don't know if I'm staying or going. I do want to go back to school but I know that the depression is going to make it just as hard to function as it has been for the last two years. I don't think anyone really understands how crippling it gets. I'm so lost. I want to do the right thing for me and everybody else but I don't know what that is. I don't even know who to ask? I want to ask Aunt Jessica but she's so busy and so far away. I hope she knows how much I love her, even if I do go. It's not fair to her or Uncle David, all they do is help and I'm sure they won't be even halfway expecting it. The idea of going back to school immediately overwhelms me but I still have a little hope in that area. I miss my friends, and being on my own with a door that locks. It may sound naive but I really think that a husband could be the one thing to save my life. Love Electra

### AUGUST 15, 2000

I've been feeling very down on myself lately, although that may be the wrong term. Perhaps I'm simply being realistic. My summer job has brought me to the point of doubting my ability to raise my own children and that is truly catastrophic. As usual, I don't know what my next step should be and the uncertainty is maddening. Things just aren't going well, and I have no one but myself to blame. If I weren't so stupid and spineless I wouldn't be so miserable. And it's not like there's anyone to talk to who could help me. What a mess and I can't help wondering if maybe God has brought such sadness to my life as punishment for prior bad acts, or maybe as a sign that I should take the plunge. Right now I feel a noose tightening around my neck. Please God send me a sign of things to come. Just tell me what to do. Love Electra

### AUGUST 16, 2000

The futility of the situation is becoming clear to me. I want to leave this place but I am trapped in that I have no place else to go. And it no longer seems worth it to stay for Aunt D's sake. She clearly values me only as in an object of unwanted coddling. But I have failed myself in that, at twenty years of age, I am still at the mercy of those who don't value my opinions and more importantly my feelings at all. It is a sad place to be in and I'm afraid that the answer I did not want to choose is becoming the only one left for me. It's a terrible thing but in the end at least I came to a final decision. I work and nothing comes of it. There's nothing I can claim is my own because there are much larger hands taking the credit. I have no parents who are obligated more or less to see to my basic needs. Instead I have an aunt who sees what she gives me as a weight to throw in my face when she's displeased. I do know what to do but somehow I don't think I have the strength to do it, to look down into the abyss and force my feet over the edge. Everyone thinks they know what I'm thinking and who I am but so few of them have cared enough to ask and really listen. How could I abandon Seymour and our future? It's kind of like seeing that the next gap is too far to jump and giving up even if it means disgracing yourself. Oh God I don't think I can do it. After all these years I've really lost my nerve. But it can't be because there's nothing else for me to do. Love Electra

# Chapter 9

# Pretender

August 20, 2000

People are starting to worry, or at least Uncle David is and possibly Aunt Ellie. I just figured out that her worry might have been her motivation for calling last week. I don't know what clues I'm giving but I'll have to stop. I'm struggling to stay functional now. The depression is taking over my life it seems. I'm not sure if I should go back to school with my mental health in such bad shape but I will because I couldn't tell them why I shouldn't. I'm beginning to realize that my desperate loneliness stems less from being trapped here in terms of alternatives and more from having no one to talk to. I really don't want to go back to school but at least I'll have my friends to help keep me sane. My family, with few exceptions, is not too objective to help me. I guess I just feel that taking this problem to any of them would mean losing control of the situation, which is true. I'm not prepared to let that happen again. So instead I'll suffer in silence and die quietly. Life has overwhelmed me in so many ways. My hatred of Phillip is still eating away at me. I've tried to get over it but the wound won't heal. I'm still not over losing Mom and I'm mad at myself for that. And to make matters worse, I'm getting more stupid by the hour. What am I going to do? Love Electra

August 21, 2000

My situation is getting harder to hide. I'm starting to look as sad as I feel, maybe as a result of my having run out of Luvox a few days ago. I really don't like being so dependent on that stuff but my body just can't do normal things on its own. Aunt D. was asked out by some guy in a jag. I'm happy for her but it just makes me realize how big a loser I am. I don't think I'm worth hanging onto. Phillip was the first person mean enough to spell out how worthless I am but I guess I've known it for some time. I don't want to hurt anybody but I don't want to stay, at least not in my current state. So what am I supposed to do? Nothing would be fair to all parties involved. I just wish I'd never been born. What was the point of this life? I haven't accomplished anything. I haven't been any help to anyone so what was the point of creating me? If only I hadn't chickened out and got caught last time. With no allies the chances of my surviving are slim as they should be because I'm not doing anyone any good here. Love Electra

AUGUST 23, 2000

Thoughts of the children I long for but don't feel able to hold on for fear of so much sadness. Getting through each day is becoming a huge challenge. I can't concentrate for very long and I lose my temper entirely too easily. I don't know what to do. Nobody believes me when I tell them that the Luvox isn't working. I'm also a little concerned by the paralyzing pains that keep shooting down my arms. Not that I can ever complain to the doctor again. They probably think I made up that whole diabetes insipidus thing last summer. I wish it had been because I have enough trouble sleeping without having to pee twice a night. It's a bigger problem than it seems, the whole sleep issue. I'm literally tired all the time. It makes everyday life just that much more difficult. I shouldn't sit here feeling sorry for myself. I should just jump and get it over with. I'm not doing anyone any good here. If only I weren't such a coward. Then I could at least do something for the good of my family. No one wants a stupid bitch even if they think they do or at least say they do. Love Electra

AUGUST 24, 2000

There are reasons for the things that happen in our lives aren't there? There are reasons why people translate lack of book smarts into a complete lack of common sense. I never really realized how little they thought of me until my disastrous college years. Aunt D. preaches as if she had any idea what was going on in my life. I don't tell her because she never helps things. I am as usual completely unsure of how to get out of this ditch in the road. It may seem cowardly to blame depression for all of life's troubles but it's true in my case. I didn't work hard enough in oceanography but I worked my butt off in management and marketing and I still did terribly. I guess the big stupid truth has finally come to light. Common sense and being a nice person won't get me anywhere. And that's all I really have going for me so I guess I'm going nowhere. What a sad existence I've come to lead. It's my own fault for being stupid and cowardly. I should just get it over with this whole dying thing. Suddenly I don't think too many people would care. Well I guess they'd care but in the long run they'd be better off. No stupid people to take care of. Why can't I just jump? What am I so afraid of? I guess I'm afraid that Mr. Right will come galloping by the day after I do. I so desperately want to be a wife and mother and I think I'd be a good one despite all my problems. I just don't want to do this anymore. Everyday just gets worse and worse and sure there are up times but not enough to be worth sticking around for. The depression that has taken over my life is simply too strong. It will eventually crush me if I have to keep fighting it alone. The truth is that I'm tired of fighting it. Tired of others not understanding it. Tired of hating myself, and my life. I may not be book smart but I do have enough common sense to know that I'm not going to be able to accomplish much depressed and alone. If I were just a little more courageous I could put a stop to this. But instead I'm afraid and so I'll stay here and hurt over and over again. Nobody here really likes me so what's the point of sticking around really? Just stop being a coward! Love Electra

AUGUST 31, 2000

And so the sad saga continues. I've lost Seymour and Brutis now. Brutis died on Monday probably because of me, and Seymour had to go back to Arlington because Amy Pollock found out about him. I sent her an email completely embarrassing myself trying to make her understand how important he is to me and she made me feel about an inch tall in response. At least now everyone's expecting me to lose it. But as I've said so many times before there will be no more attempts, the act will be done completely and successfully next time. Now I really don't have any reason to stay here. Seymour doesn't need me anymore. My family will be better off without me. It's just a matter of the how and the when. I've been hanging onto the hope that things would eventually turn up but this latest blow has made it clear that they won't. I'll never speak to Amy Pollock again but I'm still a complete loser in this situation. There's no one to help me. Kelly is being such a great friend but she'll soon tire of me just like last year. It's time to start planning. From here on out there's no easy way to turn back. My God I'm scared. Love Electra

OCTOBER 29, 2000

It's a lonely time for me here at Hill. I'm once again feeling very isolated. I know part of it is that I'm out of Luvox. And part of it is that I feel so not in control of anything in my life. The only friend I have who I think generally likes me for me is Les and she's so hard to reach now that she lives in the high rises. I know Maureen likes me but my primary function in our relationship is as an earpiece. And Kelly, well she has to be in the mood to have me around which she generally is not. It doesn't feel very nice. We are such completely different people in some significant respects. She could never know what it's like to be me. I'm tired of battling for my sanity. I just want to be normal and have a boyfriend. Why is it too much to ask? Mom would have helped me learn how to be normal or charming. But here no one cares enough or knows enough to help me. Of all who could have died why did it have to be her? I could have survived without anyone else, and she definitely could have survived without me. So why didn't God take me instead? Why has he left me in these painful times without anyone to turn to? I have always relied on my friends to keep me from falling too far but there's no one here to do that. I sincerely wish that I had never been born. It would have saved me a lot of pain and made so many lives so much better. But now twenty years later I'm still trying to justify this existence. Even if I can't do that I just don't want to spend it so desperately lonely and disliked. Love Electra

NOVEMBER 11, 2000

Yet another night spent Luvox free and falling into the background. Scary how often I find myself wishing that I'd succeeded the last time I half tried to die. This weekend is Cohen's birthday and it's shed some light on the fact that Kelly can get into such celebrations, she just doesn't care to sometimes. To be sad about absent birthday and Christmas presents so long after the fact is sad I know but I'm still stuck on the message that was sent with those. It all comes down to the fact that I am entirely unimportant in everyone's lives, including Kelly's, which is why I can't let her know that I'm breaking down again. She'll just think I'm pathetic like everybody else does. My friends don't care and my family is tired of me, not that I blame them. As we walked back from Cohen's informal birthday celebration on Friday, I realized exactly how unnecessary it was for me to be in that position. That world of boyfriends and friendships just to enjoy each other's company has never welcomed me. I guess it comes down to the fact that I seem destined to be tossed aside at some point in favor of the more important characters in this world. I am unimportant and I am disliked so what future can I possible look forward to? Love Electra

FEBRUARY 27, 2001

I guess this entry has been a long long time in the making. The depression has so completely swallowed me that I've been too listless to even write in here. I take my Luvox everyday and I've stopped cutting myself although the urge is strong. Kelly is making me feel like crap as usual but I can't break away. I'm trying to confide in Leslie but part of me doesn't want her to know how pathetic I am. I can't do anything school related it seems. I can't concentrate in class, when I study or basically anytime I need to. I just don't know what to do. There's no one I can turn to for help at this point. I hate to say but at this point if I had a real opportunity to commit suicide I probably would. I guess this is how it started the last few times. Hoping for an accidental death so that I don't have to do it. Slacking off in school. I just can't seem to get motivated. Isn't the Luvox supposed to help me function? If so it's not working. I'm just getting worse. I don't want to spend my life like this. People wonder why I can't look into the future with hope. How can I hope when it's a struggle to get through a day without wishing I were dead. This is no way to live. I don't know why no one understands that. I should write to the Hemlock Society for advice. Maybe they could help me. Maybe they'll know how to escape from this madness. Love Electra

MARCH 20, 2001

My passionate love affair with Leslie is over. Okay I'm being melodramatic, our friendship isn't really over we just discovered some rather unpleasant things about each other like the fact that I can be pretty bitchy at times and she gets pretty damn annoying after a while. I don't really understand how someone who calls me a bitch without hesitation can feel that she is justified in freaking out anytime someone teases her. I've never had a friend that I've had to tip toe around, well except Maureen. That's one of the reasons I don't hang out with Maureen that much. I love Maureen dearly but I can't live with her. Now I don't really want to live with Leslie. Two days into the trip I knew that. The accents and the shouting just got on my nerves more and more. I don't think I have a high tolerance for silliness. It has made me realize why I'm such good friends with Kelly. We're both kind of quiet but kind of silly at times. Why can't I find a nice supportive friend who isn't a racist or obnoxious? I think I'll just stay away from her for now. Anyway, something possessed me to go off my Luvox during the trip mainly that I'm almost out and figured that I'd need it more here. I got so depressed it was frightening, actually I still am. I'm completely overwhelmed. I'm starting to think that April might be a good month to die. It comes in waves but they're getting distinctly more frequent. I hate my life and I hate myself and I just get worse and worse as time passes. I have no autonomy and yet I feel completely alone. That was one of the themes of the trip. I was incredibly lonely.

I am a lot of the time. If only there was a way out of this place. Not only have I lost hope but I don't even see any possible happiness in my future. I just want to die. It may seem like a terrible thing to want but there's no longer any reason for me to live so it's only logical that I should die. My biggest fear is that death won't be any better. What do I do then? Love Electra

MARCH 22, 2001

I'm still rather distraught over the Jamaica trip reverberations. Right now I don't even want to be friends with Leslie. I'm sure it will pass but realizing that she's not my new best friend has made me even lonelier than I already was. In a way she was my lifeline to balance. I guess it was never meant to be. I've unwittingly been playing second fiddle to Vera for the duration of our friendship, as I should have realized after noting the care with which she buys gifts for Vera compared with the lack of thought put into mine. Then again she did try to get me that bear I've wanted for my birthday and that is definitely something. I just don't know how to handle our relationship in my life anymore. Who knew growing up would be this hard? God I need a boyfriend so badly. Actually I need a husband more than anything. I just don't know how I'll ever find one. Love Electra

MARCH 24, 2001

This is perhaps the most depressing loss since mom died or maybe since I lost Patricia although that was completely different. I feel so foolish for having thought that I had found a new best friend. Everyone leaves me eventually so I don't know why I'm surprised. I just thought that Leslie was that friend you're supposed to meet in college that you stay friends with forever who helps you over the rough spots. This is tearing me apart at the worst possible time. I've always prided myself on my ability to read people but this is a case where I was so wrong to think we could be best friends. It was incredibly stupid of me and, next year, I have to live with her and two people I don't know and one who doesn't particularly like me. I don't want to survive until next year, more importantly I don't think I can. There's no place I want to be right now: not at school, not at home, nowhere. Aunt Deborah is becoming quite a pest. Some people just have no idea when others are in the mood for their antics. Am I the only person that tries to abide by these things? If someone doesn't seem in the mood for chatter I shut up. I don't get offended I just respect that and silence myself. I need to be around someone who will care enough to do that. I'm so damn lonely. Why won't God send a drunk driver my way? Love Electra

APRIL 3, 2001

I knew I'd find a way to end this. It was right in my *Writer's Guide to Poisons*, a book I've had for years and now I have several options. Unfortunately none of them are particularly pleasant. It's just a matter of getting my hands on the right kind of flower. I'm trying to think of the consequences of death. Aunt Deborah has so smothered me that I'm losing my sympathy for the pain it would cause her. Leslie would be sad but she'll be fine. The bigger issue now is that my plan be infallible. The consequences of another failed attempt would be unimaginably dim. I'd probably find myself committed and that would be the end of even the possible. If the possible should die it will be because I did, not because I got caught trying to. I just looked through the entries I wrote last summer only to find that nothing has changed. I should have jumped when I had the window. It seemed like everyone was expecting me to. Now I have no window, only a bunch of flower names that might take me away. I guess I shouldn't let it be too obvious that I'm plotting. I'm just tired of asking if I will ever get better. I have two diaries full of the same questions. It's been more than five years since I started asking it. The answer quite obviously is no. It's just the coward in me that's kept asking in order to not have to face the obvious answer. The calm I feel is even scarier than the depression. It's the same feeling I get before every attempt. But this time I'll do nothing hasty. This time it has to work. I have to leave and no one can know it until I'm gone. They can't ask me to endure a lifetime of failure and pain. Somehow I'll make it out. I have to. Love Electra

APRIL 5, 2001

I'm in an odd place now. Part of me still wants to die but, more than anything, I'm just numb right now. It's rather frightening to be this way and I feel like I'm losing the ability to read my own emotions. It's stupid I know but I'm starting to regain some of my depression habits like being extremely nocturnal, as well as irritable and bipolar and irrational to some degree. I need a new depression medication. I don't understand why no one sees that. The Luvox puts me on a minimal level of functionality but it isn't helping me get my life back. I know that I shouldn't expect too much from a drug but I don't want to be minimally functional. I want to be normal. Oh well. I'm exhausted; it's definitely bedtime. Love Electra

APRIL 8, 2001

Had a fun night with Maureen, Matt and Michelle, compulsively spending of course, and putting off some major decisions though still numb and still scared. I've just realized that if I'm going to die it has to be before I move into the house next year. Killing myself there would be a terrible thing to do not to mention a terrible risk. Surrounded by that many people, I'd be bound to get found out. I hate to taint Aunt D's apartment by dying there but I may not be able to do it any place else. Les forced me to kind of admit that I have something of a thing for Dave Schind. What a joke, like he'll ever date me. Oh well, I'm just not going to let this turn into another Osama. I do at least want to be friends with him. I wonder what death will be like. Once I found a surefire method that won't hurt too much I guess I'll find out. I don't know if I could jump out of a window. That would be pretty scary. I don't know how people do it. Maybe if I closed my eyes and walked forward but I think I'd chicken out if I looked down no matter how much I wanted to jump. I miss my mom. Sometimes I wonder if I always will. If only I had died instead of her. My death wouldn't have mattered much and maybe her talents would have gotten her somewhere she deserved to be. Love Electra

*She wanted to live. She wanted to enjoy her life and the people in it. She wanted to feel love, happiness, and joy while she wrestled with the shear constant pain that every, and any life challenge brought her. She took the time and energy to write of her life's ambivalence believing that, one day, someone would figure it out. Her ambivalent message: not to deceive, withdraw, and end up like her, but to give people a chance to help by telling and talking, openly and honestly. She had learned early on that telling the truth could make her feel worse, even ashamed; her mother's response to the abuse she reported confined her to the pain of having to pretend it never happened. Writing was the only safe way to communicate her pain without being rejected or betrayed again. Electra had a profound relationship with her diaries because writing was blameless; it was hers and hers alone. Her words were her.*

*As she grew up physically, the wounds from her childhood froze her emotional growth in place and time. Adolescence for many people is ripe with life's ambivalences as identity challenges endure tattoos and body piercings, dye hair unnatural colors, experiment with drugs, experiment with people, experiment with life. Parents endure the transformation praying for safe passage into a law-abiding, tax-paying adult that even procreates in the name of love and humanity. Many teenagers have thought about not being alive. For the toughest transformations, some go through periods of deep sorrow, deep enough to consider death as a remedy for the pain of their sadness. The difference between the pain of normal life transition and Electra's pain is the degree; through near obsessive introspection she nearly brainwashed herself into believing that death was the only answer to her problems. Reality constantly challenged her self-hypnosis, which is why the process took so many years to over-take her. Tell a person anything enough times and she will start to believe it.*

*She could not internalize happiness, as much as she wanted it, even envied it as apparent in those around her. She could not understand her inability to feel the beauty of life, the beauty that she read about in fiction novels, the beauty others told her about. The beauty she could not understand was in relation to others, especially her family. From the parent she internalized, hatred and expendability became part of her from the beginning. She never developed her own identity because it was never safe to do so. The sense of self that is self-sustaining and naturally evolves from a nurturing parent bond, never developed within Electra. Her mother did not know how to take the lead in preparing Electra for life without her; even as she was dying Julie joked with her daughter about their future together. Pretense was what Electra saw often from the person she loved most. So pretense was what she modeled.*

*And all the while she pretended to be happy to her friends and family, Electra festered her mother's hatred and her father's rejection without fully understanding where these eroding feelings came from or why they tortured her daily. While never fully conscious of the source of her self-hatred, she was very conscious of the constant pain it caused her. She wanted to be a writer and she was. Through all of her secrecy and pretense, Electra wanted to understand why she suffered so much. The answer for her was the diary that became the book she always wanted to write.*

*There is only one thing in this world that every child is entitled to have, a loving parent. Children with loving parents experience the ideal in terms of God's ultimate design for humanity. But ideals aside, a single adoring, protective, and committed parent brings hope to a child's future. There is no adequate substitute, not even a large extended family. As hard as they try, grandparents are not able to replace loving parents. Children reared by grandparents still long for and eventually seek out their parents. Aunts and uncles are even less apt to fill the void made by absent parents. Often, there is no choice when parents are not around, and family tries to fill the void. Children make do; some do better than others. But, even in a most loving home, without the parent, all will long through life for the absent parent, be it absence through death, abandon, neglect, or all three. Electra never understood why she was compelled to put her intimate thoughts on paper; perhaps she had a secret hope that others would understand better than she did and do what is necessary to avoid ending up feeling the way she did. It must have been a struggle for her to write while suffering so much. But she did.*

*There is a voyeuristic desire to read the contents of suicide notes. It is often the first thing people ask about when told that someone committed suicide. As if hoping that a note will explain why it happened, what caused it, and who, if anyone, is responsible for driving the person over such an edge. But most notes are sadly brief, explain little to nothing and lend no understanding as to why. People like Marilyn Monroe, Freddie Prinze, Virginia Woolf, Abbie Hoffman, Cris Chubbick, Kurt Cobain, and others left brief one- and two-sentence notes before taking their lives. Perhaps they believed that their fame explained their actions. Perhaps fame had nothing to do with it and they dared not expose their secrets lest their fame fail to survive their death. For the many others, like Electra, there was nothing to lose by exposing the complex web from which they found it impossible to escape alive. Whether famous or not, people who are emotionally troubled are prone to copy the behaviors of troubled people like Electra. It would defeat the purpose of this book if even one copycat occurred. There is no glory here. Troubled people should talk honestly to family, friends, and professionals who can help them remedy their conflicts with life-sustaining measures. Electra was a troubled person who used suicidal obsession to try and solve general life problems people face every day. Troubled people like Electra need a different kind of help, beyond basic counseling; the kind of help that proves very challenging to even the most credentialed of experts.*

*Many people suffer from depression but most live and thrive. So what makes depression in the person who suicides so different? The main difference rests in the character type of the person who endures the depression. And character is shaped by childhood experiences. For Electra, her susceptibility to death over life may have been supplanted when the freezing cold surrounded her naked newborn body just after her mother glared into her searching eyes, put her in the crib with no blankets and buried her in the darkness behind a closed bedroom door. As people, more than 55 percent of the way communication occurs between adults is through nonverbal means. When adults communicate with children, 90 percent is nonverbal, and with babies, adult communication is almost all nonverbal. Babies are highly sensitive to internalizing nonverbal actions and inactions: grimaces, stares, touches, grunts, tones, positioning. So much more than most adults realize.*

*Is it any wonder then, why Electra still loved her mother so much? The answer is that abused and neglected children often do. Their mistreatment becomes fused with their identity as they grow into young adults, resulting in either acting-out their abuse by abusing others, acting-in their abuse by abusing themselves, or some combination of the two. In either case, self-esteem develops with such fragility that any threat to it jeopardizes hope, and life needs hope.*

MAY 11, 2001

Tomorrow, or rather today, I'm going to see most of my college buddies for the last time. I don't think it's completely sunk in that it's all over. No more dinners with friends or listening to my CDs. For the pain to have outweighed all that I'm leaving behind is amazing, but it has. I still can't believe that I even considered telling Leslie. I guess it was the part of me that wants to live, trying to get help. But there are no signs indicating that I will be pardoned from this death sentence. I'll die alone, which I guess is appropriate considering how lonely I've been in life. If I were a better person maybe I could live, but being an overall failure is pointing me toward death. And there simply isn't anything good enough about me to get me out of this. I can't spend a lifetime crying into pillows every night. But at least I'm getting to say good-bye. My plan has gotten a little more elaborate. I'm going to down a bottle of Tylenol before hand. The pain of acute liver failure will certainly send me out the window if nothing else will. Just a bit of insurance against my own cowardice. I guess it's a waste in some ways because they definitely won't be able to harvest my organs, not that a sixty foot drop was bound to leave anything to harvest; twenty-one years old and on my way to death's door. I guess I should have just done this right after mom died. It would have saved a lot of people a lot of guilt. Love Electra

# CHAPTER 10

# Never Born

MAY 12, 2001

And so I said goodbye to my college friends for the last time. Leslie is now somewhat curious about what's going on with me, but I can't tell her. I still can't believe I was ever planning to, what a disaster that would have been. At least this time I shouldn't manage to screw it up, won't wake up in a hospital again, just won't wake up I guess. But it will probably be another week before I go. I'm not sure of what I'm waiting for but I guess spending some time at home will be nice. I'm pretty calm considering what I'm about to do. No use crying over such things. That's what you do when important things are lost. I just don't know what's wrong with me. Why don't guys ever like me? Not that it matters now. But it just bugs me. I mean I know I'm not pretty, but I'm not the ugliest girl in the world. Or at least I don't think I am. I guess this dry spell has really made me give up hope. It's not the only thing but it's one of them, that and feeling expendable and lost and alone. I guess it's a good thing that Les and Russ are together now. Now I know that she doesn't need me, not that she ever did. At least I'm not leaving her alone. And I guess that it never should have mattered too much because I have obviously seriously overestimated the role that our friendship plays in her life. It was a lifeline to me but nothing special to her, which should not surprise me because that seems to be my lot in everyone's life, utterly expendable. I bet that a lot of people feel that way with their friends, but with no parents, it's just unbearable. I've fooled myself into thinking that my father not loving me had nothing to do with me as a person but it's not true. And one must know that being expendable as a daughter, not to mention a niece, denotes serious character flaws. So the countdown until I go continues, and I'll continue to wonder why God even bothered making someone as useless as me. Twenty-one years of using up resources and for what? I've been thinking about going since I was nine or so. And twelve years later I curse that child leaning over that ledge for not ending it then. Love Electra

MAY 16, 2001

I'm fairly certain that I'm bipolar now. You should have heard me a day or two ago. I was actually happy, although it was a weird kind of happy. It was more giddy than happy. That's how I imagine being high would feel. But now I'm back to my usual cheerless self although I've really been up and down all day. I'm still seriously considering suicide although now I'm feeling really really bad about what it's going to do to Aunt D. I also really want to go to Madonna's concert. It's always been my dream to see her in person. It would be great to do so before I go. But that's certainly not the best reason to stick around. I'm still feeling so bad and so afraid. I don't know if I can keep hanging on for anybody, not even for me. That might have been twenty years from now. I'm not even so afraid of the fall down anymore. Life is terrifying by comparison. Decision time is coming up fast. It's really such a shame that it has to be this way. I certainly was some legacy for mom to leave. You can't really leave a legacy that can't survive without you. Love Electra

MAY 17, 2001

I don't know how I managed to convince myself that I could go for a few days without Luvox and not be affected. I'm in no state to make the decision about whether I live or die. At least my head is clear enough to realize that. My hands are so shaky. It's frightening. But I guess that's okay, definitely not the worst symptom of the depression I'm dealing with. I'm just afraid that this is related to something besides the depression. Of course there's nothing I can do about it. I've already overfilled my quota for mystery ailments. They must all be in my head because nothing is ever physically wrong with me. I guess I'm just strange in that respect. Grandpa sounds like he's losing it. I so wish that I could bring grandma back for him. I wish that my death could mean something. I wish that I could give my life to some dying person that wants to live. But unfortunately they won't let me sacrifice my life to give up my organs. I just wish that I could be a good thing for someone. I wish that I had been good enough to help some people out during my lifetime. Maybe I'd be worth saving if I weren't sleepy all the time and so shy. I hate being shy. Maybe things wouldn't be so bad if I could reach out to people, but now I'm heading more toward agoraphobia than anything. Please God help me stay alive. Help me reconnect with the rest of the world. Just show me what to do. Love Electra

MAY 19, 2001

Almost got into a bad conversation with Aunt Deborah. Not an argument or anything just an awkward conversation about my mental health. It's not like I can tell her that I'm cracking. I think I'm still going. I feel terrible either way. The best reason I can give is that I'm damaged goods and this should be returned to my sender. I can't live constantly missing my mom. I can't go on hating Phillip, it hurts too much and yet I can't let go of it. Most of all, I can't go on hating myself. I have no self-confidence, and a person can't succeed without that. I just need to go. Being lonely all the time does bad things to you, as does depression in general. My body is starting to react negatively to it too. I so wish that I had gotten this over with right after mom died. It just gets harder the longer I wait. I feel so awful about this but I just can't do it. The future has dimmed any hope I had. Grandma will die. Aunt Deborah will get some nasty cigarette related illness. Uncle David's health will spiral downward. I think that I was too cold towards Les. I was just feeling sorry for myself, and trying to reach out. I'm not mad at her I just think that I've lost her, pretty quickly too. Which goes to show that even to my friends I'm completely expendable. Love Electra

MAY 20, 2001

Well the first argument has occurred, of the summer that is. Not angry just annoyed is all, getting increasingly annoyed because her TV is blasting and the door is locked so I can't turn it down. This is what will push me over the edge. Sometimes living here is just so irritating. I may keep my date with death on Tuesday but I'm still not sure. It might be later, but it won't be much later if things continue as they have. No great loss to the world but I do hate to hurt my family like this, especially those that aren't expecting it. Not that I'm exactly an integral part in their lives either. It's a confusing time in my life. I wonder if anyone thought I could really make it to adulthood. Because I think it's been obvious for years now that without help I wouldn't. At least this way I'll get to be with mom. I can't believe it's been almost six years since she died. I still miss her terribly. Just can't get over it. It's the eternal grief. It has gotten easier to deal with but I'm still not handling it well. Wish I wasn't such a loser that way it might be worth dying just to see her again. Of course I'm not sure of that part of death but there's no other way I'll ever see her again, well at least not anytime soon. We were meant to always be together. She understood me so well. No one else does at all, it seems. Love Electra

Who am I trying to kid with this hope for a future? Even if I weren't so depressed, there's no escaping the terrible performance I gave last semester. I couldn't concentrate so I stopped trying. It happens every semester, dumb thing to do but not surprising given my track record. Nevertheless part of me is fearfully clinging to life. Not sure it wants to stay but afraid of going. I don't know how to make this pain stop and I don't know who to talk to. Even confiding in Dr. Vasa brought me grief. If you can't talk to a therapist about such things who are you supposed to turn to? My friends all have other things to worry about. Then again I am a master at hiding things so there's really no reason for anyone to know that something is terribly wrong with me. Even if they did see, who could or would help me? Going might be the best thing for me not to mention for everyone who has to deal with me. Besides, every time I open up to people nothing good comes of it. A mentally ill orphan doesn't have much to offer this world. No one wants us around anyway. Just crawl under a rock and die and you'll be okay. The battle is over and you've lost just as we knew you would. Love Electra

MAY 22, 2001

Today is supposed to be my last day. I'm still not sure I can go through with this though. I really want to and I really don't want to. There are so many things I don't want to miss. I want to have a family and go see Madonna. But I don't want to be depressed anymore. And I don't want to be lonely anymore. So what do I do? It's rainy and cold outside right now so I'm thinking that tomorrow might not be a good day, today that is. What good is a person too shy to express themselves? I'm too unappealing to attract people without words. Face it my life is going nowhere. I know they say that every life is precious but mine seems pretty worthless. I just have to make a choice. It's a difficult task but no one else can do it for me. Elizabeth was the only person I've ever known who could ever be objective on the subject. If she happens to hear that I've gone, she'll probably understand why better than anyone even though we really haven't spoken since high school. If I could do it with pills and be sure that it would work, this would be so much easier. But I can't try and fail again. I'll be institutionalized not to mention disowned by my family. This is why I can't talk to them. They'd just get upset and ask me to explain what I'm feeling in terms of what they want from me. I've heard their stories of coming to the brink but I'm not convinced that any of them have been this far. We're in shark-infested waters. A big wave will definitely be the end of us. So in a way it's in God's hands. I could really use a really blatant sign right now. Just tell me what to do God. A glimpse into my living future could settle it but I'm not sure anything else could, except a husband, of course. I wonder if Sylvia went through this. Love Electra

MAY 23, 2001

An interesting turn of events, first it was pouring outside which postponed my fall because for some reason I really don't want to go in the rain. Then, Aunt Deborah sprained her foot so now I can't go until she's better which will probably mean staying for another week or so. It could be a coincidence or maybe it's a sign of some sort. I've been very irritable tonight. Even Seymour's driving me crazy. I so wish that I didn't have to go like this. Jumping out of the window was the last method I would've chosen to use if I had a choice. I don't want to do it but I can't risk taking a bunch of pills and waking up in the hospital. Even if I used prescription painkillers, which I will soon have access to thanks to Aunt D's foot, there's still a chance I might live. Tylenol would kill me, but it would take an unpleasant while for that to happen. If only I had a gun or curare or something like that. All I'm sure of is that there cannot be another foiled attempt. This time I must succeed. I'll keep working on a method but for now I have to stay put to take care of Aunt D. I think she may be starting to suspect something. I wish I could cheer up and allay her fears but it's just not in me. I can barely keep it together at all, but alone well not that she can do anything about my mood anyhow. No one can help me out here except God of course. I've been granted a short stay of execution a call from the Governor might come in yet. Love Electra

MAY 24, 2001

Surprisingly, things are looking up. Uncle David seems to have found me a well paying job. I thought I was going to end up working at Giant again. But now I'm in a bit of a quandary. I was only planning on living until yesterday and I've acted accordingly. So what should I do now? It's no reason to die but it will make things unpleasant next semester and for the rest of the summer. I'm still not sure that I'm going to stay. I probably won't. Things don't generally go well for me over long periods of time. I'll just have to try extra hard to keep my head above water. I don't know if the struggle is worth it but I'm not giving up just yet. Although I have to admit that a major drama would be the end of it for me, like pushing over a man on crutches. Mom's birthday is in a little while. I hope it's not too hard to get through. She would be forty this year. How cruel it is that she never reached this birthday. It so should have been me. I'd take her place in a second, although I probably wouldn't be in such a miserable state if she had lived. God, I loved her so much that it became part of who I am. I miss her so much even though it's been six years almost since she died. How can a heart need someone so badly? It's really working against my survival. But then I've always known that loneliness was my biggest roadblock. It is always present and does so much damage to my psyche. I can only keep praying for a husband. I hate myself for being so shy but it really is crippling. A husband might help me regain some self-esteem and then maybe I wouldn't be so shy. But since I am so shy my chances of finding a husband are minimal. It's in God's hands. I can only take things one day at a time because any more completely overwhelms me. I just keep wondering if my whole life, however long that may be, is going to be like this. It's no way to live. If this is what it's always going to be like then maybe I should go now. Love Electra

May 29, 2001

Today Phillip came up again. The mention of his name invokes such horrible feelings in me, such hatred. I don't like feeling this way. I'm still in limbo over this whole suicide thing. Really not sure I want to go and equally unsure that I want to stay. Phillip makes me want to go. Aunt Deborah's foreseeable health problems make me want to go. Grandma's deterioration makes me want to go. Feeling like I have no place in this world makes me really want to go. It looks like my family is going to go up in flames eventually. I don't want to cause it but I also don't think I can bear watching it happen. Besides I'm damaged goods now. I live life in constant fear of rejection. Feeling completely isolated all the time is no way to live. Most of all right now this house thing is overwhelming me. I realize that a large part of my depression is constantly feeling overwhelmed. My head is never far enough above water to feel safe. I haven't felt safe since the March '99 incident, maybe ever since mom died. I just don't think I can get through life. I think I'm not well equipped enough to deal with things everyone else can deal with. I'm so tired of being afraid and isolated. But I can't seem to break free of these horrible feelings. All I can do is try to take things one day at a time. I wish I had some idea what the future holds. Being so unsure of things just aggravates the situation. Love Electra

MAY 31, 2001

Aunt Jessica of all people called tonight. It always makes me feel good to talk to her. If only I wasn't such a numbskull about calling her. I know she's so busy all the time. I don't want to be a pest. I'm considering passive suicide, taking unnecessary risks, that is. I so don't want to hurt my family, most of it at least. But I don't think I'm going to make it. I think I've outstayed my welcome on this planet by at least six years now. And the damage done in March '99 pretty much sealed my fate. I can't live being suspicious of everyone's motives for everything. I certainly can't live not being able to feel secure in any relationship in my life. This goes beyond low self-esteem into the realm of the psychiatric illnesses. I wonder if there's a drug to remedy stupidity and paranoia. Aunt D is giving me a hard time about taking Seymour back. If I was dead at least she could have him. He's one of the few things that really make me genuinely happy. And of course someone's trying to take him away from me. Story of my life I guess. It was good hearing from Aunt Jessica but it just made the choice I have to make a little harder. I don't want to do this to her. I love Aunt Jessica so much. I love all my aunts so much and most of my uncles. But I can't take these bad feelings anymore. I wish Elizabeth were here. She would understand but no one else even tries to. They make these presumptions about your motives for wanting to die without even stopping to examine the problem. Some seem to think that you can just turn off these feelings when you really want to but it's not true. I can't turn them off and they never go away. It's like being trapped in a cage with a gorilla that's always screaming and body slams you every once in a while, usually without warning. It never goes away and sometimes it really knocks you out. What's more, it's pretty obvious that if this creature doesn't stop hitting you eventually it's going to kill you. This is my world, horrible as it may seem. That's it in a nutshell. Love Electra

JUNE 1, 2001

Had a bad day for no particular reason. Those are the worst. They just showcase your mental illness. I am stressed about this furniture thing and this house in general. I already wish I were living on campus next year. But no one would stay with me and so I am now involved in a house that is completely overwhelming me, not that it takes much to do that. Did some research and discovered that electric accidents are not the way to go, although at the very least the pain would be brief which is a plus. I'm just not sure that it would work. I guess if I got shocked in a bathtub I'd probably drown. Oh boy I really do have to decide whether to stay or go. I don't want to hurt my family and friends, such as they are. But I don't want to live out a miserable lifetime either. The family is clearly tired of dealing with me, and my mental problems so I can't turn to them for help. I have to deal with this alone, besides I know from experience that sharing these problems with them only makes life more difficult. And Dr. Vasa showed me exactly how untrustworthy therapists can be. Even if they could help I can't trust anyone to see the illness for what it is as opposed to taking it as a personal insult, completely alone. But that's been true since mom died, although I wasn't aware of it during certain stretches of time. I've just been so foolish and cowardly in the past. There can be no more attempts at suicide. I have to either succeed or not try at all. I don't want to do this to Aunt Deborah but I can't stay. I don't belong anywhere with anyone. It's just so lonely in my world and it's eating me alive. I'll keep pondering this. I wish I had some idea of what the future holds. How can everyday life possibly hurt this much? What happened to me? When did I become such an incredible loser? How did this get so bad? Love Electra

JUNE 3, 2001

The house is coming along nicely. We drove up there to deliver some of the furniture. It was stressful but I didn't fall apart or anything and Aunt D only went into super bitch mode once and came out of it relatively fast. This doesn't mean that I'm staying though. Being a fat jobless lonely person still hurts. I feel like I'm constantly on the verge of tears, like any little thing could push me over, literally. But then I've already picked out the names of the four girls I want to have. But then maybe I wouldn't even be a good mother especially since I cannot be on antidepressants during my childbearing years. Why does life have to be so complicated and why can't I have a husband? Maybe I'm too frigid. I guess I can be sometimes when I get into my dark don't come near me moods which is often. Being fat and stupid and ugly doesn't help things any. Maybe Phillip is right. Maybe I am worthless. And maybe there is no chance of my amounting to anything. Each day I just sink further into the muck that is my life. I should just end it all. I'm going nowhere or worse fast. I might as well save myself the trip.

JUNE 4, 2001

Another down day, I've been tired for no reason and my mood is swinging like a pendulum. I wish I could just get a grip but I never seem to get a firm hold on things. I seem to have lost all control over my life and it feels awful. I haven't spoken to Aunt Ellie since I got back from school and I'm not sure why. I love talking to her but something is holding me back. Perhaps it's fear that she'll be able to see through my happy facades. Or maybe I don't want to have to lie to her about how well things are going. I'm not sure but I guess we'll touch base eventually. I'm definitely leaning towards suicide right now. I can't see any light at the end of the tunnel. I'm so easily overwhelmed that it doesn't look like I'll ever be able to function as an adult. The means is the most bothersome point. No more attempts just death for me. No more being accused of using my suicidal tendencies as leverage to get what I want. All I want is to get out of here. That's all I wanted the first two times. If I weren't so stupid I would've gone a long time ago to join my mother where I belong. I'll try to hang on to life until after Aunt Jessica's visit. I want to see her again. I hate to hurt her this way because she has done nothing but good things for me. Funny, how those who will care the most, have contributed the least to my downfall. Not that anyone but me is responsible for my apathetic existence. Love Electra

June 6, 2001

I finally saw Aunt Ellie and the kids. It was wonderful but I think she may have noticed that I'm a little off these days. I'm planning to cook a fabulous dinner for Aunt Jessica and Uncle James next week. It may be the last time I ever see them. It will be hard saying goodbye. Aunt Ellie showed me pictures of Phillip's kids for some reason. It was an unpleasant experience. I just don't want to even think about their existence anymore. It's the only way I can deal with the March '99 incident. Two years later and it still hurts to think about it. I'm still kicking myself for not succeeding then. If only I had done a better job. I feel like I've just been falling down hill ever since. Three years of living with Phillip taught me to be lonely and really hate myself more than anything. At least I can go, knowing that most of my cousins will grow up well. They barely know me anyway. They all have parents who love them. They all belong somewhere. I haven't had a place in life since mom died. It's pathetic but it's so true. Love Electra

June 7, 2001

I have said many silent prayers for Niki Taylor, a model who I don't know and probably never meet. It's just that she's a mother with everything to live for. And it just makes me wonder why death can't be more fair? People like me should be able to die young in place of others who have no choice. I'm sticking out these last two weeks so that I can see Aunt Jessica but after that it may be time to go. Aunt D seems tired of me already. I guess it's because I'm too much of a loser to find a job. Honestly I have been enjoying my leisure time. I really needed to take these four weeks off for my sanity. But I know that it can't last and soon I'll have to go back to the real world where I'm a complete failure with no one to talk to. It seems like it's always going to be that way. So I should leave. Aunt Ellie has done such a good job raising her children. I hope she knows how much I love and respect her. She probably won't come to my funeral, if they even have one for me. She'll just be mad at me for going. She doesn't know how hard it's getting just to smile sometimes. Eventually everyone's just going to get tired of me anyway, damaged goods is what I am, not valuable at all and crushingly lonely. It's an ever-present weight on my spirits. It's my own fault for being so shy and stupid. The ugly is completely my fault. People have no trouble throwing me away because I am trash, worthless trash and how can trash have any good place in the world? I just have to stop being a coward and go. Love Electra

JUNE 8, 2001

I think I should have been born a cat. I'd be better suited for that kind of life than this one anyway. I envy so much of Seymour's existence I think I love him a little too much. Should I outlive him I don't know what I'll do. I can feel myself sinking now. I'm sleeping more during the day and staying up later at night. I'm always having bad dreams and I wake up every few hours. I just have to hang in there until after Aunt Jessica's visit. But even that's been harder than I thought it would be. I spoke to Nicole today for the first time in ages. Despite what Phillip the arrogant jerk thinks, I think she really is an intelligent person. It really is a shame that her morbid obesity is most likely going to kill her within a few years. I wish God would make her healthy and take my life instead. She has a little boy who needs her. I wouldn't want him to turn out anything like I have. How did this get so awful? Was I always this worthless, I wonder? I mean what was the point in my ever being born. I've never served any purpose in life. I've always just been some unfortunate person's burden not to mention my own. This is why I hate myself, and why I was thrown away by Phillip: because I am useless and stupid and irritating, because having me around is like having a piece of rotting meat in the middle of the room. Nothing good comes of it just bad things. Occasionally I manage to kid myself into thinking I have some potential but I don't. Maybe I never have. Maybe I mistakenly thought that some of the light emanating from Mom was actually coming from me. But I don't bring light. Parasites never do. I can't be a coward anymore. I am trash and trash is only good for throwing away, nothing else. I thought a husband could recycle me but I don't even have that kind of potential. He probably wouldn't love me anyway, or at least he wouldn't after a while. Everybody tosses me into the garbage can eventually, so I have to go. Love Electra

June 9, 2001

As preparations for Jennifer's graduation go forward the family is already starting to talk about mine. They couldn't possibly know that it's not going to happen because no one but me knows that my life is drawing to a close. I'm very sad about it. I think that at some point I had a lot of potential, before Mom died of course. And despite all of the scary events of my childhood, I did have a good life back then. It shouldn't have ended this way. Mom shouldn't have died at thirty-four. I shouldn't have let myself drown like this. I certainly should have recognized that I was never going to be loved or wanted in Baltimore. How could I have been so dumb? A lifetime of lessons obviously didn't teach me much. I was too stupid to see that I was always going to be alone once mom died. So I guess I deserve to die. It'll be just like taking out some particularly foul trash. I hate to do this to Aunt D and the rest of the family but I'm not worth fighting for. I just want to be with my mom again. She was the only person who ever made me shine on my own. How do you get over losing someone like that? A better person might be able to but not useless trash like me. All I can do is pray that God will give me the strength to do what I have to do: a mercy killing of sorts that has been a long time coming. Love Electra

June 10, 2001

There are certain things I just don't get. Aunt Karen is one of them. Sometimes I think she hates me and other times she treats me like I'm exempt from scorn. She generally shows over family. Uncle David is another mystery. I know Aunt Deborah can be annoying at times but he jumps on her whenever she says anything. Quite frankly I don't think that he likes her very much. I also don't understand how Jennifer can seem so oblivious to the fact that her mother seems rather oblivious to her. That family could be so wonderful. All the ingredients are there but together they just don't mix well. It makes me think that even if I had been raised in a so-called normal family I'd still be a failure as a person. Not that it matters much now. My life is essentially over, and has been for some time now. I promised myself that I wouldn't go until after Aunt Jessica's visit but I'm not sure that I can wait that long. I guess I'll just have to resist the urge until after this weekend. At least I'll manage to show that much control. If only I weren't so afraid. Love Electra

JUNE 11, 2001

We spent the day with Jennifer at an ultra boring awards show where she didn't win. But at least she seemed to be having fun and she looked great. I kind of feel like I'll be passing a torch on to her when I go which I think will be early next week. My few remaining hopes and dreams will die with me but for the most part they're already gone. I'm receiving some not so subtle cues that the family expects me to make up with Phillip. They're obviously unaware of the fact that I am barely past vehemently hating him, if at all. I never want to see him or his family again so the chances of our making up are minimal. I'm not saying I did the right thing in the situation. I should have either succeeded or not gotten caught at the very least. But he'll never really know how much his actions destroyed me. Maybe after I'm gone he'll think of such things but even then he probably won't realize that a big part of why I'm going is that living a life constantly in fear of another rejection like that one has finally put me out. In a way I started self destruct-ing two years ago. I've spent the time since then trying to cover a messy injury with old band-aids. I'm simply worn out. No energy left, no strength to fight off the depression, and this time I'll succeed. At least that's one thing I'll do right. Love Electra

JUNE 12, 2001

Having chest pains today. I didn't even realize I was stressed out. Depressed yes, but not stressed out. Aunt D. is really good to me and I'm going to repay her by temporarily ruining her life. The fact is it's become a struggle to get through every day. I have no desire to do much of anything now. So few things appeal to me anymore. It's like the inside of me has al-ready died and is just waiting for the rest of me to catch up. The thought of going back to Penn alone makes me want to die. I really do hate it there. Actually, it's possible that in my current state I'd hate it at any college. This pain just never goes away. It hasn't completely left me once in over six years but now it's unbearable. This is why I've come to the conclusion that death is my only option. I so wanted to have kids and get married. But I feel like I've got the mark of Cain on my forehead. Like everyone can see what a reject I am and that I am one to discard. The whole family is really going to hate me for going, except the Florida relatives who just won't care. I probably won't even get a funeral. That's probably for the best because there aren't enough nice things about me to fill a eulogy. Love Electra

JUNE 13, 2001

Chest pains have gotten worse and I still don't know what I'm going to do with myself. I really don't want to die, but I don't know what else to do. Two stints in the psych ward and months and months of therapy have done little to alleviate the depression. A slew of antidepressants also haven't worked. Prayers, trying to open up to friends, and using quantities of alcohol haven't worked. I'm starting to think that I can't be fixed. I guess that's what Phillip knew. Just throw it away instead of trying to fix it because it's a waste of time. A tough pill to swallow but in the end there's no point in denying it. I'll just try to get through the next few days. I just hope that she doesn't sense that anything's wrong. She'll hurt a lot when I'm gone but good people like her don't deserve disastrous nieces like me. It will be so hard saying goodbye to her and the rest of the family. I don't want to do this. I want to stay with my family and friends and Seymour. But I can't live like this. I can't be sad all the time. I can't hate myself all the time. I can't live and not even be functional. The loneliness is just too much and it never goes away. I can't live a life constantly fearing that those who profess to love me will discard me if I mess up. And I'm always messing up. I'm such a failure as a person. People only throw away losers. Love Electra

JUNE 14, 2001

Tomorrow, or rather later today, is Jennifer's graduation. The divisions within the family will be very obvious there. Aunt Ellie and her family won't even be there. It's very sad to see this happen to the family but all the involved parties are at fault here and no one is willing to apologize. Aunt D is only making things more tense by nagging Uncle David about his attitude toward grandpa. If there's anyone less receptive to nagging than I am, it's Uncle David. He really has very little tolerance for it, which isn't good considering how much our family does it. I'm very afraid for him these days. He is a heart attack waiting to happen. At least going will spare me the pain of having to live through that. I'm still in a state of complete turmoil over what I should do about that. It's all so hard to deal with. I just feel ill equipped to handle life's challenges and there's no sign of things getting any better for me. I'm too stupid to use all the gifts I've been given for anything productive. Instead I've managed to get stuck behind every speed bump that's come my way. I'm no good to anyone so I should just go. But I'm scared and sad about giving up my future. I just don't know what to do. Love Electra

JUNE 15, 2001

Aunt Jessica finally came today. She didn't seem terribly excited to see me but that is to be expected now that I've relinquished favored niece status to my younger prettier and less troublesome cousins. Just another sign that it's time for me to go. Even Aunt Jessica won't care that much so it's only my cowardice that's keeping me here. How can a person be so spineless? Eventually I'll get up the nerve. I happened upon a card William gave me (after my bureau tipped over this morning) detailing the danger signs indicating suicidal tendencies. I fit the description to a tee. It's too bad William's gone back to England and I'm beyond help anyway. It's just too late for me it seems. I've let myself go to the point of no return. And today at the graduation I realized that this family really doesn't need me. Maybe it never did. It is strange enough to go on without the likes of me being around to mess it up. I just have to get up the nerve to do what I have to do. How can someone with such a big loving family possibly feel so desperately lonely? It's such a bad feeling and it never goes away. Love Electra

JUNE 16, 2001

Spent the day cooking dinner for Aunt Jessica and company. The meal went nicely. I guess I was just being my usual stupid self yesterday because Aunt Jessica was definitely happy to see me. Which makes what I'm about to do just that much worse. At least I got to say goodbye. Jonathan hasn't changed much, which to me is a good thing. How ironic that I'm just starting to really appreciate my family just as I'm preparing to leave it. I still don't know if I'm going to have the guts to do it. I'm still as afraid, and a little voice inside of me keeps wondering if six stories are enough to kill someone. I think it is but I'm not sure. I know eight is and I know nine is but six doesn't seem like that far. I have to be absolutely sure that I'm going to make it out of here or else I'm not going to do it that way. But I don't know of any other relatively painless way to go. Six stories have to be enough or else I could wake up in a padded cell. There can simply be no more attempts. Whatever way I go I'll have to figure it out soon I think, maybe after this weekend. I did what I promised which was to hold on until after Jennifer's graduation, but maybe now that that's over I should go ahead. I still don't want to die. But I do want to find some peace in life and I just can't seem to get there. I still can't believe this is happening. I just want this pain to end. Why is that asking too much? Love Electra

JUNE 17, 2001

I think I may have unintentionally hurt Aunt Jessica's feelings last night with my side comments about the larger guests at the Dinkins family reunions. I have nothing against fat people but I'm definitely more inclined to joke about them than any other group. I've just never thought of Aunt Jessica as being overweight. I know she is but she's my aunt and it never mattered to me except in the context of its toll on her health. Anyway I just hope that I didn't stick my foot too far into my mouth. Tonight she stopped by just to give me some spending money. I thought that was so nice of her. It still saddens me to think that I might never see her again. I seem to be losing this battle with the depression. Instead of learning to cope with the constant despair it has just continued to eat away at me. Perhaps there's nothing here worth saving. My family is going to hate me once I'm gone which I guess is better for them than missing me terribly. I just have to keep telling myself that they'll be better off without me. It's not that I don't believe it. It's just hard to consider having people you love so much, hating you. I guess I'll just have to get used to the thought. Maybe my death will bring some estranged relatives back together, although I may just be overestimating my importance in their lives. There's no easy answer to the quandary I'm in right now. I'm always sad and it's hard to think straight in such a state. Love Electra

JUNE 18, 2001

Do you know what it's like to have no hope and no motivation to do anything? Instead of living each day like it's my last, which is always a possibility, I keep sinking further and further into the muck. Maybe it's just that I'm out of Luvox. It's amazing how quickly I fall down without that stuff. I hate having to pop a pill just to stay sane. I've been on that stuff for more than four years now and not only can I not function at all without it but I don't even function well on it. So I'm screwed either way is the basic gist of things. I just have to stop being a coward and go. I hate to let Phillip win like this but I am running out of strength and time. Being a loser is no way to exist. I so don't want to hurt those members of my family that actually will care when I die. Today was so bad Aunt D. was driving me crazy. She doesn't care how miserable I am as long as I have a job, and getting a job is difficult when you have no skills as I do. Why can't I just end this? There's no point in my staying. I don't want to hurt my family but I can't stay either.

I don't know what to do and there's no one I can talk to. What am I supposed to do? And the thought of jumping out of the window terrifies me almost as much as the thought of staying does. It's a problem with no right answer and all the outcomes are so wrong. I pray for an answer every night and nothing seems to come of it. I know God does things on His own time but I don't know how long I'm supposed to wait for relief. Or is the lack of a solution a sign that I'm supposed to go? I just don't know and what if I survive the fall? Is it possible? Is it likely? I have to get out of this somehow, but how? And when? God please help me. I can't do this alone. Love Electra

JUNE 19, 2001

Still here, obviously, my main concerns are the how and the when. And the, is there anyway to make this less painful for my family. Truth be told, I don't think there is. They're going to hate me either way it seems. The how is still a big problem. I don't know if I can bring myself to jump, at least not while sober. Aunt D. will be out Friday and Saturday night so that might be a good time to go. In fact that may be the opportunity I've been looking for. A bottle of wine should give me the nerve to go through with it. Wow it's really over. I'm sad but relieved. My stomach is turning itself apart with the horror and the stress of all this but there will shortly be no more of that. Electra Juliet Montier Binet will die this weekend at the age of twenty-one. Six years later than she ever should have been. Phillip may be winning this battle but at least I'll finally be at peace. No more dealing with jerks like him, and no more living in fear of rejection. And at least I won't have to watch myself sink into the depths of manic depression. And the people I leave behind will be better off without me even if they never fully realize it. I can't be happy about this though. I wanted to have a family. But I'm not fit to be a wife or a parent anymore. I'm not fit for anything anymore. Love Electra

JUNE 20, 2001

Interesting turn of events, suddenly I'm employed. I'm not sure of what that means for my plans. I'm not quick to attribute things to Divine intervention but talk about interesting timing. So now I'm not sure of what my future holds. Suddenly I might have one. I don't think so but at least it's a possibility now. I'm not going to get my hopes up. But it might pose a problem if this project lasts past Friday. I'm supposed to go Saturday but I don't want the temp agency to look bad having someone they referred suddenly become unavailable. Overall I guess, it's been a pretty good day. We went to my new favorite Italian restaurant and I worked out. Aunt D. is harassing me about picking a career. I wish I could just tell her that I'm not going to be around long enough to have one. But that's not going to happen. Interestingly enough we were talking about how far a human can fall without dying tonight. I'm still not sure that sixty feet will do it but I guess if I go down hard it will. There's no other place for me to do this and I don't have access to the roof. It's still a pretty risky method, but I guess it's better than inducing liver failure which sounds like a miserable way to go. I hope mom is waiting for me wherever I end up. I don't think I'd be contemplating suicide if she had lived. Perhaps I'd be just as miserable, but I don't think so. I certainly wouldn't be as lonely. Why was I such a coward after she died? I should have gone then. Love Electra

June 24, 2001

Well I blew it again. I was alone most of Friday and Saturday night but I'm still here. The only half-hearted justification I can give is that I want to finish my summer job. No reason they should be inconvenienced by my mental defects. My horrifying thought is what if I never get up the courage to go. I can't stay and if I can't leave I'm even more screwed than I was before. I have to find a way, a sure fire way. Why won't God just take me in place of someone else destined to die young who wants to live? If only it worked that way. I'm struggling to die while better people are struggling to live. How unfair is that? I just have to go. I can't forget about my family but I can't stay like this for them either. Even now when I have a good job I'm still miserable. I just seem to be beyond repair so why bother trying? Love Electra

June 28, 2001

I'm once again unemployed and exceedingly irritable today. Aunt D was badgering me about my post graduation plans and wants me to pay seventy-five dollars a month in room and board fees. I guess it's only fair but it's just one more thing I have to stress about. I protested which I'm sure will get out to the rest of the family thus increasing my reputation as a parasite. I honestly don't know why I'm still here. I know I can't stay and yet I can't make it out of here. I don't have anyone to talk to here, not that I really did in Philly either. No one really cared there either. I just need to go and be with my mom. Aunt D rarely fails to either generally annoy me or make me feel worse about myself. I love her to death but I would not want to live in a world filled with people as intolerant as she is. I find it disturbing that someone as imperfect and unempathetic as she is, thinks she can judge people and their motives. Her prejudices bother me more than they should I know but it just highlights the great divide between us. How could I ever confide in someone like that, who represents values I abhor? I know that I'm about as far from perfect as you get but I do try to keep myself from stereotyping people. I don't want to be judged by anyone's actions but my own and I try not to do it to other people. Lots of good is done. I'm still alone. Love Electra

JUNE 30, 2001

I am living in an apartment with someone who is quite possibly the most annoying woman on earth. It's not that I don't love Aunt D because I do. It's not even that I don't like her, because I usually do that too. It's just that she seems to think that bothering me is of absolutely no consequence. I know she doesn't see how I feel but how many times does one have to say go away before she'll listen. I have to get out of here. Not just here but out of this earth. I hate to leave Seymour but I guess he'll be all right. At least her smoking has given me a good reason not to stay for her. I mean she's killing herself with the cigarettes and not watching her diet at all. So I am definitely not sticking around for her. I'm so sick of depending on other people. But I'm too useless to support myself so the best answer is just to die. I wasn't destined to amount to anything anyway. I'm still not sure of why God bothered with me in the first place. Seems like He would have been better off saving himself the trouble. No point in making something useless and unattractive. Oh well at least I haven't had any children to screw up. Love Electra

JULY 3, 2001

So many nightmares, I'm not sure what to make of it. Usually I'm looking for mom, but I never seem to find her. My life is such a mess right now: jobless and friendless and hopeless. My time is definitely fast approaching. Too bad it has to happen this way. I say that as if I knew how and when I'm going. Well the when part isn't too hard, the answer is simply, soon. How is a bit harder to figure out. I'm so afraid of jumping but I don't know how else to go. If only we lived in a higher floor or at the very least on the eighth floor of the building. Then I'd be guaranteed a ticket out of here. I guess that's a chance I'll just have to take although I'll be praying the whole way down that I don't wake up paralyzed or worse. The summer's half over so I don't have much time to waste. This whole thing makes me so sad. But alas that doesn't matter. I have no friends to speak of. My family will be better off without me. And I know that Seymour will be taken care of. I'll get to be with mom, hopefully. I won't have to watch grandma deteriorate anymore. Aunt D. will be parasite free. Life will go on no worse off for the lack of me.

So I just need to quit feeling sorry for myself and go. I will too, as soon as I get up the nerve. Love Electra

JULY 7, 2001

I'm so irritated with Aunt D and myself, at me for being a coward, at her for being a nag. She's still trying to push grandpa and I together, even though she promised that she would stop meddling: so much for that. I'm going through exactly what I went through last summer and the summer before that. I was completely suicide bound at the end of the school year. Now I'm home and I don't feel suicidal anymore, well at least not to the point where I usually feel it. But I know I will want to again once I'm back at school and by then the opportunity will have passed me. The thought of living in that house is almost enough in itself to make me want to go. Being this way for an entire school year would be awful. I don't know why I ever agreed to live there in the first place. I clearly knew that it was a bad idea from the start. But my life has just been a story of bad decisions starting with mom's decision not to abort me. And so here I am wedged between yet another rock and hard place but this time I don't think I'll be able to squeeze my way out of it. I think I'm just stuck and this space is only getting tighter. The Luvox isn't working. My mental health is declining and I don't know where I can go for help. The whole situation is just awful. And I'm so useless that even the temp agency can't find work for me. This is the worst I've ever been, I think. And my moods are shifting like a pendulum. I just want Aunt D to stop nagging me. So what if I function better at night and like to stay home. That's the least of my problems right now and her nagging is just increasing my stress level. But she never sees it. Love Electra

# Chapter 11

# Awake

July 14, 2001

What am I still doing here? May was supposed to be my last month but I'm still here, and still miserable. I'm trying so hard not to let anyone know but even that is beyond me. A trick I used to pull without even thinking about it is now the hardest thing in the world. And it really doesn't matter anyway because I'm beyond help. I don't look forward to much anymore. I'd just like to sleep all day and play on my computer all night. What is clear is that I can't stay. Too much dealt, too much failure. I've just lost the ability to cope with anything. And there's no one to talk to anyway, no real friends in the world, no husband or children. And so it seems that this, the sixth anniversary of the day my life ended, would be an appropriate time to go. The depression runs my life now. I've lost control. And I've been hoping for something, anything to hold onto but there isn't. I'm miserable at a job with nice people and an easy task, so what hope do I have for ever being happy in the real world? I'm so tired all the time. I can't live like this anymore. I just have to go. If only I had the courage. I just don't think I can jump no matter how much I want to. But then I don't want to endure an agonizing death either. What am I supposed to do? I don't know and I'm running out of time. School starts in less than two months but even that would be overtaking my resources. I don't even want to face getting up for work on Monday. I so desperately need help but I fear that God has abandoned me. I just don't know what to do. Thirty-two thousand people come to this point in America every year. I just don't get why this has to happen to us. I'm living on serious borrowed time here. I just have to figure out how to end this. My research has come to naught but there has to be a way. Love Electra

July 17, 2001

When will I free myself from this hell? I've really settled on a method this time and I have two possible times; one is tomorrow, which is unlikely. The other one is in a week and a half. I'll have a whole day to myself, and it will probably be my last. I know that I've been irritable lately but Aunt D is driving me crazy. It's like being the pet of a big bullying child with Down's Syndrome. I've lost my right to solitude and quiet. Add job stress to that and you've got the reasons behind my incredibly frayed nerves. I love her and I usually enjoy her company but she never listens to me. And her moods sway between puppy dog and bitch like a pendulum. I know I do the same thing but at least I usually know when to leave someone alone. What a way to end this life. I realized today that I miss my grandmother. She really had more layers than we ever got to know and, unlike Grandpa, she didn't let the bible think for her. He's a good man but very one dimensional in a lot of ways. Maybe it's for the best, as it seems that the more layers you have the more ways there are to get hurt. Maybe that's why Phillip leads such a charmed life. It's time for me to start counting down, as I don't have much time left. Love Electra

July 25, 2001

This particular house of cards is quickly crumbling. My Capital One debt has come to light after I lied about it for fear of being severely judged. It was stupid of me but then what else is new? I got a new computer yesterday, which I thought would make the difference. But then Aunt D spent the night yelling at me while I tried to fix a frustrating problem because she clearly thinks that I'm some kind of moron when it comes to computers and everything else. It just made me realize that nothing material is going to help me through this. It's just time to go and I cannot deny it any longer. I'm not functioning well here, and the thought of going back to Penn makes my blood run cold. I feel terrible about doing this to the family but I think that they'll do better without me dragging them down. I'm just so tired of it all. And I can't deal with school again. At least I'm not a complete failure at work, which is more than I can say for my Penn career. Love Electra

August 18, 2001

It's been a while since my last entry and not because I didn't need to write. I've just been avoiding committing my current misery to paper. I have no business still being here this close to the end of the summer. I just haven't been able to bring myself to jump. I have to admit I am more than a little scared. But it has to be done, and the coming school year fills me with more dread than the fall does. I'll make it out there eventually. I have to. Things aren't going so well with me now and they'll only get worse in September. I have to tell everyone at work that Aunt D is my mom, which makes me feel terrible. They're nice people but I can't strike up any real friendships there because the first nineteen years of my life can't exist for them. And what kind of daughter would pretend that her dead mother never existed? What kind of horrible person would do that? I loved my mother more than anything and yet I've betrayed her everyday, just one more reason that I don't deserve to live. And I won't. If I have to drink Drano and die in agony, die I still will. Love Electra

AUGUST 30, 2001

I'm sitting here at a crossroad of sorts. I have to go back to Philly on Friday or I have to die now. And even at this late hour I still don't know for sure what I should do. I want to die but I don't want to jump out of that window. What am I supposed to do, spend an entire miserable lifetime for the sake of my needy aunt and the rest of my family? I just don't know. I hate my life. I hate myself. And my inability to do this is just making me feel worse. It's not that I don't want to. I just don't want to go like this. But I can't bear the thought of going back to school especially living in that house. I can't face that. So I have to be brave and go. There's nothing else I can do. I just have to make myself. Oh God, I'm so scared. I've finally proven that all the material things in the world can't make up for an utterly miserable existence, spoiled rotten but too stupid to function in the real world. Oh please, God help me. It's never worked before but I'm praying for help here. But I guess even God has abandoned me at this point. There's no one who can help me. Phillip was right; I'm not worth the trouble. Love Electra

SEPTEMBER 1, 2001

Still here both alive and in Arlington, still don't know if I'm going to make it out of this apartment alive. We're going to Philly tomorrow but I just can't live there. And so I have to decide how to end this. If I'm going to be a coward perhaps death by liver failure is what I truly deserve. I can't stay even though I am loved and have all the material things I want. I am not fit for life, too stupid and unhappy, too irritated. Aunt D is driving me up the wall, constantly whining and always worrying. She takes no one else's advice and is drinking herself into an early grave but we're all supposed to listen to her. Give me a break. I need to be numb so I can do this. I have no control over this life and everything I've done in it has been wrong so why would I even think that there's a bright future ahead of me. I try not to judge people and to give them the benefit of the doubt but this family always says I'm wrong and, at the end, I'm still done. I'd live if only I didn't have to go back to Philly. Then I might be able to keep it together but I can't bear being alone in another's house. At best here I'm kind of safe. And for all the nerves she's frazzled at least I do enjoy Aunt D's company most of the time. I just can't go back to Philly. I hate it there. But I have no say in the matter anyway. I can't sponge off Aunt D for the rest of my life and I'm not good enough in any sense to find a husband, just plain useless. That's why I have to go, one way or another. Love Electra

SEPTEMBER 5, 2001

Let it be known that I tried. Couldn't make it out of the window so I downed 12 grams of acetaminophen. All I got was a stomachache although I haven't dismissed the possibility that the results will later be known. You can survive with only part of your liver functioning or something like that. So hopefully I've at least done some damage. We'll see how that goes. I'm in Philadelphia now. My room looks great but it can't make up for the fact that I am utterly done here. Out of the nine people living in this house, I'm the only single one. Although by now I should be used to being lonely. I'm starting to feel invisible. I try not to think of it as the state I'm always going to be in, but it's hard to have any hope: nobody's best friend, nobody's girlfriend, not important to anyone but my cat. And even not to him for any reason other than that I feed him. Can't live, can't die. What could God possibly expect from me, just one stupid ugly, lonely girl with no future and an exceedingly painful past, nothing special, or at least not in a good way. People die every second. Why can't I get out of here? There just has to be a way. Love Electra

DECEMBER 15, 2001

Optimism is always succeeded by disappointment and failure in my life. I had such high hopes for this semester but I was stupid to think that I could ever be anything but my lazy stupid self. So it's August all over again except now I live on the second floor instead of the sixth so, even if I weren't a coward, I'd still have to find other means. Apparently my friends think I don't need a boyfriend or anyone. I have an air of self-sufficiency, meaning that I can fail on my own. What the hell am I sticking around for? None of my friends care about me. I'm just comic relief. And half of my family hates me.

I'm useless. Do you know what that's like to have no place in this world, no purpose and no hope? It's killing me inside and sometimes I can't even hide it. I can't even write well anymore. It was the only talent I had and it's gone. No more of this, I'm begging you, no more loneliness, no more pain. I just want to be normal and whole. I just want my future back. Love Electra

JANUARY 1, 2002

This has become a familiar pose for me: sitting on my bed contemplating my death. Only this time is a little different, as I've actually taken steps to get there. I was stupid to think that a coward like myself could ever jump out of a window even if six stories were desperately lethal. So I'm going with the plan I botched back in '99, except I'm using chloroform instead of sominex. It took a lot of courage to order it. I don't know how I can explain it away if anyone finds it. Not that they should, but just in case. There were so many things I wanted to do, but I find that there's a brick wall in my path that I can't even see the top of. I'm stupid, unattractive, depressed, charmless, and a compulsive spender. I've had a while to examine the letter and I figure that I feel compelled to accumulate things because they are the only happiness I have a lot of the time. This thing with grandma is so overwhelming. I miss her in a way, but more than that, I hate seeing her so degraded, just like mom was. Those images still make me wince. Grandma's condition makes me feel doubly bad for being such a burden to my family and a general failure. It's been more than I can bear for a long time. I hope this stuff arrives soon, and God I hope it works. Love Electra

JANUARY 7, 2002

Annoyed, very annoyed. Guys in my life are just getting on my nerves. They just never stop; never treat anyone that's not thin like a human being. And some of them, i.e. Russ, don't live here and yet never leave. I was just meant to be alone, or not alive. Even Seymour is getting on my nerves. I wish the chloroform would come. I've even stopped doubting the necessity of my dying. It just has to be. But that won't be for at least a couple of weeks. For now, I'm exhausted and I can't go to sleep because of the noise from downstairs. I don't even know why I'm so tired. It's just a constant burden on my shoulders. Who can I talk to anyway? Even normal things have flown up in the air. The first of this month no rent check and no messages from anyone. Aunt D. just expects me to come up with it magically. Uncle David, of course, came through but I had to tell him at the very last minute because I thought she'd take care of it. I also succeeded in making an ass of myself this weekend by ordering four expensive drinks when Karle's parents took me out to dinner. I should be locked in a dungeon somewhere and stewed to death. I can't even pretend anymore. I just want to go away for good, no function here anyway. Love Electra

JANUARY 14, 2002
    Well isn't this reminiscent of old times, me sitting in bed with dawn quickly approaching quietly contemplating my impending death. Except this time I think I will actually succeed. Granted I thought I would succeed the last time and the time before that. But in retrospect that was stupid of me. How quickly they (my family that is) all forgot how sick I am. I've told Aunt Ellie and Dr. Prinz that the Luvox isn't working but no one believes me. It's no joke that I'm on this stuff and still suicidal. But no one who might see it cares enough to look. And lord knows I'm not going to bring on that kind of humiliation to save this pathetic soul. Besides, the future just isn't looking too good for me, or my family. Grandma is dying. I'm convinced that Uncle David is eating himself to death. I'd be devastated if he died, and constantly worrying about him is just stressing me out more. Aunt D is a lost cause. Uncle David might lose the weight but I don't think she can make up for two decades of smoking. I don't want to outlive any of them. So I have to go. It's just terrible, I know, but unavoidable nonetheless. Love Electra

JANUARY 17, 2002
    I cried through the last episode of the Mary Tyler More show even though it aired three years before I was born. It seems that I can't even face leaving my TV friends. I think that a lot of my emotional problems stem from the constant fear of being abandoned, not surprising given my track record. I'm still waiting for my deliverance (the chloroform) and I'm having a lot of trouble holding it together in the meantime. I've lost the ability to act normal or, if not the will, the strength. I just wish it would hurry up and come so I can end this. I don't want to outlive any more relationships. So I'm sleeping all day to avoid dealing with this anymore, I guess. I'm just so tired all the time. Not that that's anything new. The one unresolved problem when it comes to my death is what to do with Seymour. I guess Aunt D will take him afterwards but what do I do with him during it? I'd feel bad leaving him trapped in here with my body but I certainly can't leave the door open, and he needs access to his box and food and water. It seems murderous, but I need to take care of him before I abandon him. At least I know he'll be in good hands, and hopefully I will be too. Love Electra

FEBRUARY 14, 2002

This has been an interesting day. How appropriate that tomorrow, or actually later today, will be another lonely Valentine's Day. On one of the few days that I wasn't wondering about it the chloroform came. And no one knows but me. I thought for sure I'd get caught, that something would get in the way. But now I have a clear path out of here. I also diagnosed myself with Borderline Personality Disorder based on what I've read on the web. It may seem like a shady source but I read the description and it was like reading the story of my mental history, even the cutting, which I'm doing more and more now. I'm still going but at least I have some idea of what's wrong with me. I'm not even pretending well now. I've been to one class this entire week. I'm sleeping more and drinking more. And yet no one seems to have noticed, or at least if they have they don't care. I don't think that the magnitude of this package has hit me yet. I'm really going to be free. I feel terrible for leaving this way but I can't stay. I'm just a burden on my family anyway. I got so many of the right ingredients: a loving family and good friends. I'm at one of the top schools in the country. And yet I'm still too stupid to make it work. This world is definitely better off without me. That's why I'm always alone on Valentine's Day, because I'm garbage, a curse to my family and friends, even my cat. I'll be sticking around for another week or so to watch the figure skating competitions at the Olympics but after that I'm gone. Love Electra

FEBRUARY 17, 2002

It's not so much fear but a pervading sadness that haunts me as my life draws to a close. It is sad that I will never have children or even see my twenty-second birthday. Don't think that I take this matter lightly. Even if it wouldn't devastate my family it would still be sad that a person such as me has come and gone. But I've discovered the horrible truth about myself and that is that I have no place in this world. I'm too stupid to use any of the opportunities I've been given. I'm too unappealing to attract a male. I am simply a burden on my family and friends. And I'm not going to wait around to see how much they'll deal with before tossing me out. I've already been through that once and the fear of it happening again is more than enough to keep one from staying. I should have realized after that March that I could never survive it. It changed how I look at myself and especially how I look at other people. Now, almost three years later, I'm still recovering and now I'm spinning out of control. The cutting is back in full swing. I'm sleeping too much and drinking too often. None of the good vibes from the people around me can reach me. They're like the sun and I'm like the bottom of the ocean. I love so many people but something is so wrong with me that I can't even reach out to them. I don't think that anyone loves me enough to help me without judging me. So there's a bottle of chloroform under my bed waiting to do me in. Twenty years from now, no one will care. But for at least a month or so people might really hurt. I feel terrible about this, but I can't stay. I'm too weak and too stupid. Only a miracle could save me now. Love Electra

FEBRUARY 18, 2002

To tell the truth, the very thought of this act fills me with dread. I should be relieved but instead I'm just sad. I've accumulated so many friends and so much stuff. Unfortunately there's no middle ground. When I think of all the stupid things I've done to make this death necessary. All the compulsive spending, all the lies I've told to keep people from knowing how pathetic I am. It just makes me hate myself so much. I can't stall much longer. I owe money that I can't pay back and I've been unable to convince myself that I should still be doing class work even though I'll never graduate. I say I want to wait for figure skating but I really just want to hold on to this life for just a little longer. Love Electra

FEBRUARY 21, 2002

An uneasy countdown continues. Four short days until I end my life. The last time I tried I don't think I felt quite this sad about it. Hard to believe that was nearly five months ago. I wonder what kept me going so long. I'd hate to think that it's just lack of opportunity. I'm very paranoid about my relationships with people. I have been ever since mom died. I've just never felt secure in any relationships since then. I guess that not being secure at home was part of the problem. But at least in high school I could deal with it. After March '99, I stopped being able to cope. I held it together for so many years when mom was alive and putting me through hell. I think I used to overlook the more traumatic aspects of my childhood because I was determined to remember her as the best mother ever. She wasn't. But I don't think many of her shortcomings were her fault. And despite everything, I still loved her more than anything. She and her brother, unfortunately, pushed me into silence. I can't tell anyone that I've screwed up and thus I can't ask for help. And it's not pride that makes me that way. It's fear. I'm not sure if I ever could have lost that fear. I try to tell myself that bad grades and debt are not things to die over. But that fear makes them that significant. Not just now either. I won't be able to get a job and my paranoia has me envisioning my family abandoning me. I can't just talk to them like anyone else would. I'm so afraid of being rejected and yelled at and judged. So you see this is why I can't stay. Even if I miraculously got over this hurdle, there would only be more in my path. The only thing I want to do is be a casting director or a housewife, and I can't be either, too stupid for one and too ugly for the other. Love Electra

FEBRUARY 24, 2002

Let's be honest here. With only twenty-five hours or so to live we're not relieved or even just plain sad. I am sad but more than that I'm absolutely terrified. Not so much of dying as I am of leaving. Everyone will soon know exactly how rotten I am. But my life and my mind are falling apart. Who will really mourn for me besides Aunt D., Aunt Jessica and Uncle David? Maybe, Grandpa and maybe even Aunt Ellie although I doubt that. Maybe I'll even make it into the TV. I hope it doesn't seem callous to be planning this in advance without giving anyone warning. That's the problem with suicide. You can't prepare people for it without them backing you up in some mental ward. I can't go through that again. Or maybe they won't be surprised. I mean, do they actually think that depression like mine goes away on its own? I didn't help myself either. I should have asked for help but I just couldn't bear to. The thought filled me with so much shame and fear. So instead I stayed quiet and fell apart. It was a little more bearable in high school. I had Elizabeth to talk to at Park, and Dr. Owen and all the rest. I've never felt so comfortable talking to anyone at Penn or even in my own family. But I shouldn't have let it get so bad. I should have done something. But I didn't. And my only excuse is the knowledge that I am not worth saving. If anything, 1999 taught me that or at least set it in stone. But it started even before that I guess. I miss my mom so much. I've never gotten over that, as I should have. What it comes down to is my inability to cope with any of life's hurdles. It's time to go live out my last day. Love Electra

FEBRUARY 25, 2002

This is my last entry. Four thirty is the witching hour when I put my cat to sleep and then myself. My curiosity about what happens next cannot outweigh my sorrow over the departure. But I guess life is a test of some sort. And I have failed that test miserably. There was no miracle, just one sad girl sitting in her room alone as always waiting to depart. The world won't be losing much and, on the whole, my family will be better off. I don't mean to hurt anyone. I just can't take it anymore. My methods of survival don't work and I am too lonely to go on. A very ignorant man once told me that you shouldn't need other people. The truth is that if we didn't need each other the human race would have destroyed itself long ago. Maybe mean people like him can exist alone, even though he's never had to, but most of us don't get along so well without each other. I'm living proof of what loneliness can do to a person. Right now I'm debating over whether or not I can stay for another day. It's a bad idea but I'm having a bit of trouble letting go. I really don't want to go but I can't stay. I can't lose sight of the big picture surrounding my life. I am a failure and a liar and a coward. People like me make this world a rotten place. Well I'll have to decide soon. Tonight is the better idea. But maybe going tomorrow would be okay too. Love Electra

MARCH 7, 2002

Yes the coward's still here, still going but still here. I don't know why I thought I could make myself do this at a certain time. I've tried enough times to know that it doesn't work that way despite what some people might think. It's like a switch has to be switched, but not a regular switch, more like a dimmer. This time it's going off slowly. The last time it went off a bit more quickly. I wonder if I'll die a mystery to people. People don't know silly little things about me, like how I hate the Olsen twins to the point of destruction. Like how I make up running stories in my head, before going to sleep, that go on for months and years sometimes. Or that elderly people make me very sad. I'm an odd duck and, in many ways, it's obvious. But in other ways I'm good at hiding it. My family perhaps understands me least of all. But there are reasons for that. As a non-religious person I can't help but be an outsider to them. I don't know why it should make them love me less, but it does. I've never tried to sway any of my cousins in any unchristian direction. I've never put them down for believing things I don't believe. I mind my own business on those points and avoid discussing it but they hate me anyway. What business is it of theirs what religious beliefs I hold? It's not like the Bible was the one thing standing between me and prostitution and murder. It makes me mad but there's nothing I can do about it, no love for me just judgment. Love Electra

*As much as Electra tried to convince herself that her family did not love her, she knew that this was not the case. She could not understand why their love couldn't help sustain her but she did not take her life in March of 2002 because she wanted to see her family, her loving family, again. During her college spring break, Electra returned to Virginia to celebrate her twenty-second birthday with her Aunt D, who took her out to her favorite restaurant. She stopped by to see her Uncle David and his family, her grandfather and grandmother, her Aunt Ellie and cousins. Her visit to each relative was brief as she said goodbye before her return to Penn, as her spring break came to an end. No one knew that she had come to say her final goodbye. When she visited with her Aunt Ellie, she spoke of her graduation plans, telling her aunt to expect a graduation invitation in the mail. Her aunt saw the strain in her face and the sadness behind her smile but believed it to be from the normal stress of her studying for final exams. But the aunt saw something else more distressing; her niece's appearance was very different this time. Electra had cut her long hair and tied it back in an unusually disheveled fashion. She gained weight to plumpness from the slender frame that was natural for her. She walked with slumped posture and her clothes were tight and mismatched. She spoke with a monotone, childlike voice, looking her aunt in the eye sometimes but mostly turning away, more focused on the distance. As she left her Aunt Ellie's home during that final visit, she appeared expressionless until her Aunt Deborah made a general comment about interracial relationships with Middle-Eastern men. Electra's response to the comment was that of intense anger, accusing the aunt of being xenophobic. Her burst of anger disappeared as quickly as it had appeared and both aunts were puzzled by it. Aunt Ellie attributed the outburst to the emotional toll 9/11 had taken on public opinion since the tragedy had taken place less than six months previously.*

APRIL 2, 2002

Well I guess I always knew it would come to this. There will be no reprieve this time. My life is scheduled to end in a few hours. The rent is due tomorrow and I don't have it. And if there's anything Phillip taught me it's that my life and wellbeing are completely unimportant when compared with the almighty buck. But this isn't his fault, although he didn't help. It's my fault. I'm still angry and upset about things that happened years ago. I can't hold onto money. I'm stupid and worthless. I fall hopelessly in love with guys I have no chance with and then act foolish around them. I'm too shy, too ugly and too stupid to ever find anyone. And I'm a liar. When I'm too embarrassed or too afraid to give the real answer, I just make something up. I can't stand up for myself or ask for help when I need it. I am utterly and completely useless and ill equipped to lead any kind of productive life in this world. I just have to get out of here. The stress is making my hands shake and my head hurt. I'm sleeping and eating way too much and the worries just overwhelm me. Every time I see Aunt D light up or Uncle David eat something greasy it overwhelms me. Aunt D., she's given me everything she can and yet she drives me crazy. I just can't deal with it. And Grandma, well what can I say. She doesn't deserve this life. I miss my mom and I still feel terrible about saying that Aunt D was my mom at work. Aunt D just doesn't get it, but then I don't think she really ever tried to get it. I can't take care of my cat who needs me. I don't want to do this anymore. And I'm not going to. So I'm saying goodbye to you, diary. So sorry I never got to finish this. Love Electra

*Pain is both a universal perception and universal deterrent. Whether the pain is physical, emotional, financial, existential, or spiritual, human instinct gravitates toward pain relief in order to hold onto happiness. Despite her academic achievements and her convincing demeanor as the jubilant teenager, Electra never recovered from the pain of being abandoned and abused by her biological parents. Wounds like these never heal without powerful spiritual intercession.*

*Instead, she continued to re-experience the pain from her past every time she faced another disappointment, whether from her own sabotage or the normal course of life's increasing challenges. Her pain was also worsened by clinical depression, but her underlying personality caused her to sabotage treatment for depression and then use her depression as a weapon to hasten her self-destruction. The pain of loss was like an ever deepening, weeping wound that would not heal. Her increasing self-hatred, self-degradation, and self-mutilation were feelings and behaviors that modeled her mother's expressed emotions when she was alive. Electra was never allowed to build sufficient self-esteem that could allow a natural separation from the identities of her father or mother into a truly independent person because the nature of her maternal bond never gave her permission to safely do so. She loved her mother and would deny to her death that her mother did not love her, that her mother hated her.*

*It was from her mother that she first learned to hate herself and from her father that she learned to sustain that hatred to the point of ingesting alcohol and chloroform while completing her last diary entry, tying a plastic bag over her head and lying down behind a locked bedroom door for the last time. The chloroform she had given to Seymour did not affect him, and it was the incessant, high-pitched howling of her beloved cat that alerted her friends that something was wrong. When the police broke down Electra's bedroom door, she lay dead on her bed. Through the clear plastic bag she had wrapped tightly over her head, they could see her eyes open as if she were still awake.*

*Pain causes tunnel vision, restricting the ability to see options in life. Years of pain can color the sunshine gray, perceive smiles with paranoia, make options look like barriers, and turn happiness into guilt. Even during times of apparent happiness in Electra's life she was never able to hold onto it. There was no pill, no psychotherapist, and no person on earth that could fill her void of sadness. She was right about Divine intervention being her only hope. But the personality she grew into would not allow a journey into spiritual healing.*

Much like Sophocles' mythological character called Electra and her constant lament over her murdered father, through her life view, Electra Binet made several laments about her family losses. The way she perceived the world was as misguided as the way she perceived the family that loved her so much; the misguidance was shamefully orchestrated by her biological mother and father. She unknowingly internalized the hatred from the mother she loved and the disdain from the father she wanted. It was never Electra's fault. She was not given a fair chance, when it mattered the most. Happiness is a state of mind that she could not hold onto because it was not allowed to become familiar to her. She only learned how to pretend to be happy like the people around her.

In her young life, sadness was planted and festered by life-changing experiences. Sadness became her comfort zone because it was more familiar than the alternative. Happiness is choices, but Electra learned only how to narrow her own choices such that sadness would entrap and permanently confine her. Happiness is memories but neither Electra's mother or father imprinted sustaining ones during her childhood. No matter what challenges life brings, most people forge ahead by finding inspiration in warm, restorative memories of their childhood. The loving hugs, reading times, movies times, exchanging smiles from across the room, just being together all combine into emotional memories that sustain happiness even in times of hardship. Happiness is hope that our actions and inactions will help us enjoy future progress. Happiness is the ability to take control of those actions and inactions that help build the fabric of life. Happiness is what rescues us from disappointment and loss. Happiness is planted in the first ten years of life by parents that project the earthly image of a loving God onto their children. Happiness is God.

Electra's grandmother died of Alzheimer's disease a year after she died. Unlike the morose perspective that Electra predicted, her grandmother did not die a frightful or humiliating death, but, instead, passed away at home in the comfort of her husband's loving arms. While her seventy-seven-year-old grandfather did grieve considerably, the support of loving family and intrinsic love for God helped him heal. He still grieves over missing his wife of fifty years, but the happy memories they shared have lessened grief's sting to allow him to wear a smile on most days. Today, he goes for walks every day, takes regular vacations with family, and enjoys babysitting his grandchildren. He smiles more and more everyday because memories console him and God sustains him, adaptive strengths that Electra, unfortunately, never learned. Today, her grandfather thrives.

Deborah grieved Electra's death and then her own mother's death but did not fall apart, as Electra had predicted through her own lament. Deborah continues to be comforted by the memories of her sincere efforts to help her niece and her mother before they died. Now, Deborah is a successful businesswoman and happy owner of two cats, one of which is Seymour.

*Electra believed that she had found a special bond with her Uncle David because he financed her education without asking questions and gave her money on demand without accountability. For this she quickly idolized him and predicted that he would thrive for his efforts. But, like Electra, David and his wife discovered the hard way that everything eventually comes with responsibility, accountability, and consequences. Today, David is bankrupt. His only daughter dropped out of college and had to work three jobs to help out with her parents' financial situation. David remains a bitter man who openly criticizes his siblings for providing too much guidance to their children, what he asserts as over-controlled parenting, even while he wrestles with providing any guidance to his own children. Many parents make excuses for minimizing their involvement with their children. Some are just lazy parents who don't care to face the hard work that is required for successful parenting. Most people become parents without any guidance beyond what they experienced from their own parents. What Electra and David failed to accept is that happiness is limits and love helps guide those limits. People who fail to respect limits in their lives end up being very unhappy and making others unhappy too. Sustainable life needs balance which means setting limits on the many weights of life's journey.*

*Jessica is living happily with her husband in the suburbs. Jessica had gone back to school in her thirties and graduated from college at the same time her son did. She then went to graduate school to study psychology and learn more about her own internal struggles and how they impacted her life. Happiness is insight. Once Jessica understood the way her own mind worked, she had better insight into achieving her goals. With this new understanding, Jessica was able to help others by building a thriving practice as a psychotherapist. During the year following Electra's death, Jessica's new insight helped her succeed in a lifelong challenge to improve her ill-health from morbid obesity. She lost nearly one hundred pounds and continues to be physically fit today.*

*Ellie and her family reside in the suburbs with an older daughter who volunteers at the hospital while attending college, a son who is studying to be an engineer and two younger daughters who, like their older siblings, are thriving, balanced, and blessed. Happiness is not a passive process. Happiness takes work. Ellie and her husband are constant in their efforts to guide and interact with their children even when they push the parents away. Everyday Ellie contends with the stress of setting limits on adolescent rebellion and the pain of watching her children toil from their mistakes, always optimistic that they will learn and thrive as a result. Happiness is contagious. Happy parents rear happy children who grow into happy adults that become happy parents.*

*No one ever understood why Electra mailed a birthday card to her eight-year-old cousin before she died, as it was not her cousin's birthday nor were the two girls* close in any way. Inside the card was a cloth bookmark that Electra had treasured as a gift her mother had given to her as a child. Also inside, Electra had penned in glitter ink, cheerfully written words of "happy early birthday" and "I'll see you soon" all written with exclamation points, "xxooxx" for hugs and kisses with stickers of colorful balloons. It was a very colorful and cheery appearing card. This was Electra's last act as the pretender. The card embodied the appearance of happiness. But happiness is not tangible.

Phillip and Susan are doing well in both their professional and personal lives. Their two children are beautifully balanced and are very close to their parents. Unlike Electra's predictions through her lament, Phillip is a compassionate and involved father who constantly reassures his children with hugs and kisses in the context of loving guidance. His children excel in school, sports and, even though still in elementary school, can beat most adults at chess. Phillip and his wife provide the same loving guidance to their children as they tried to give Electra. But they had no foundation with Electra, who was already enslaved by woe when she went to live with them at the age of fifteen. Had Electra been able to accept their guidance, had she been able to put aside the damage of a well-concealed trauma, she would be as beautifully balanced as her cousins are today. Happiness is foundation. If a person grows into adulthood without ever having a solid foundation from childhood then happiness is tenuous at best. Maternal neglect, sexual molestation, and paternal rejection prevented any footing for Electra's foundation.

Electra's father, Thomas, was living with his wife and second daughter, only an hour's drive from Electra's residence at the time of her death. No one knew this before she died, not even Electra. No one knows what he is doing today, if he is parenting or neglecting his only living daughter. If he had wanted to be involved with his eldest daughter, he lived close enough to do so most of her life. Thomas was the man she glorified. He was the father she hoped would be a parent. Happiness is knowing, without a doubt, that at least one parent really loves you.

Electra left behind the ingredients of her despair. If these ingredients had not been mixed so thoroughly into her life then she would be alive and prosperous today. Now there is understanding about how the facets of unhappiness doomed Electra and so many others like her. Parents and people planning to be parents need to wake up and see just how preventable this was. It will take hard work once there is appreciation for the work that needs to be done. Parenting is harder than any other aspect of life, but, when done with love and diligence, the rewards credit human existence. Electra was so tortured while awake that she took respite from life. From the words of her soul, let's hope that we all wake up to the fact that no one else need die by their own hand. The work needs to begin at the beginning so that the seeds of happiness can be planted there too.

# Appendix

# There Is Hope in Seeking Help

Where to Call for Help

If this is an emergency, please contact your local crisis center or call 1-800-273-TALK (8255).

If you are a parent seeking help for your teenager, call Teen Help National at 1-866-460-4086.

National Alliance for the Mentally Ill (NAMI) Informational Helpline: 1-800-950-NAMI (6264).

National Sexual Assault Hotline: 1-800-656-HOPE (4673).

Statewide Family Violence and Sexual Assault Hotline: 1-800-838-8238.

For a copy of the *National Strategy for Suicide Prevention: Goals and Objectives for Action*, call the Center for Mental Health Services's Knowledge Exchange Network at 1-800-789-2647. Refer to document number SMA 3517.


Where to Go Online for Help

Take the Suicide Knowledge Quiz on the Youth Suicide Prevention Web site, http://www.youthsuicide.ca.

http://nimh.nih.gov/publicat/bpd.cfm.

http://nimh.nih.gov/SuicideResearch/highrisksuicide.cfm.

http://www.cdc.gov/ncipc/pub-res/suicide%20fact%20sheet.pdf.

http://www.mentalhealth.org/suicideprevention.

http://www.mentalhealth.samhsa.gov/suicideprevention.

http://www.surgeongeneral.gov/library.

http://www.surgeongeneral.gov/library/calltoaction/calltoaction.htm.

# Index

## About the Author

MILLIE OSBORNE, M.D., is a psychiatrist and assistant clinical professor of psychiatry and behavioral sciences at the George Washington University School of Medicine and Health Sciences. A graduate of Brown University and the Medical College of Virginia, she has more than 20 years of experience helping people and their families recover from self-destructive behaviors. A Diplomat of the American Board of Psychiatry and Neurology, she is also a Diplomat of the American Board of Geriatric Psychiatry. As medical director for a large community agency and editor of a public healthcare newsletter, she mentors students, develops educational programs on suicidology, conducts roundtable discussions for professionals, and provides second-opinion consultations. She is the mother of four children, three of whom are teenagers.